curry
101

PENNY CHAWLA

curry 101

100+ DELICIOUS CURRIES FROM KITCHENS AROUND THE WORLD

Smith Street Books

Contents

Introduction

British legend of stage and screen Tim Curry once said, 'It's good to be a national dish.' True, the United Kingdom considers its curries – an import from former colonies in the Indian subcontinent – a distinctly British affair but, unsurprisingly, they're not. Curry can mean many different things to people around the world. The word itself is an Anglo-butchering of the Tamil word *kari*, meaning sauce. A curry can be any dish, meat-based or otherwise, cooked with spices. Their sauces might be creamy or stew-like, dry or wet, mild or spicy. This book is your manual for mastering this diverse cuisine.

The recipes in *Curry 101* hail from 27 countries including Afghanistan, Bangladesh, Ethiopia, Fiji, India, Indonesia, Japan, Kenya, Malaysia, Morocco and more. Naturally, the flavour (and heat) of each curry is dictated by the produce found in its region of origin. And it would be easy to assume that the one ingredient that connects these dishes and makes a curry, well, a curry is the humble chilli. Because that's what spicy is, right? Those little red things? Wrong.

The chilli hails from Central America, a region not exactly known for its curries. There are hundreds of varieties, from the mild to the tongue-searingly hot, but it is the long red chilli that has come to adorn supermarket shelves and be known by most as the universal symbol for any food that brings a sweaty sheen to your forehead. And although you will find this chilli in some of the recipes in this book, there are a host of other peppers and local spice mixes used to give curries their distinctive flavour.

Caribbean curries get their heat from scotch bonnet or habanero peppers. Ethiopian cuisine's distinctly peppery burn comes from its berbere spice mix (see page 219). The noodly laksas and fragrant curries of South East Asia and Indonesia balance fiery curry pastes with coconut milk and ingredients such as lemongrass and galangal. The flavours of India change radically from region to region, and from one household to the next. Garam masala (see page 218) – that unmistakeable blend of cumin and coriander seeds, among other family secrets – is typical in the north. Lentil-lovers in southern India create soups that are both spicy and sour, thanks to the tamarind fruit.

One thing is guaranteed – you're going to need a bigger spice rack.

What remains constant about all these dishes is how they are destined to be shared. Multiple dishes should hit the table at the same time and include sides of bread and rice to mop up delicious juices. Then everyone can mix and match as they like. Combining flavours creates entirely new curries, right on your plate. Try pairing different curries from the recipes that follow – stick to one region for a traditional feast, or go rogue – whatever curries your favour.

The chapters are separated by main ingredient: pulses, nuts and legumes; vegetables; seafood; poultry; pork and beef, and lamb and goat. Each recipe has a heat-rating: one chilli is mild, two can get pretty spicy and three means business. There's also a chapter for perfecting different breads and rice, while the final section covers the basics for you to batch your own pastes and spice mixes.

So get cooking, you're in for a journey. *Curry 101* is your new savoury passport – go get it stamped.

DAL MAKHANI
14

CHANA MASALA
17

MASOOR DAL
18

MOONG DAL
19

DOUBLES
20

CHANA DAL
22

MCHICHA
23

MISIR WAT
24

CASHEW CURRY
26

DAL BHAT
29

Pulses, nuts & legumes

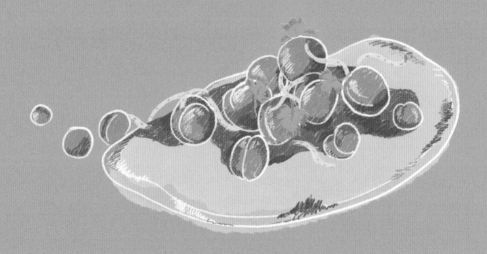

Dal makhani

India

100 g (3½ oz) urad dal (black gram),
   well rinsed
100 g (3½ oz) dried red kidney beans,
   well rinsed
60 g (2 oz/¼ cup) chana dal (split
   chickpeas/yellow split peas), well rinsed
1 cinnamon stick
5 green cardamom pods, cracked
5 whole cloves
400 g (14 oz) tin crushed tomatoes
100 g (3½ oz) unsalted butter, chopped
4 cm (1½ in) piece ginger, finely grated
4 garlic cloves, crushed
1 tablespoon chilli powder, or to taste
¼ teaspoon ground turmeric
1 tablespoon dried fenugreek leaves
steamed basmati rice (see page 178) and
   puri (optional), to serve

SERVES 6–8

Place the urad dal, kidney beans and chana dal in a large bowl and cover generously with water. Cover and set aside to soak overnight.

Place the cinnamon stick, cardamom and cloves in a square of muslin (cheesecloth), then gather into a bundle and secure with kitchen string.

The next day, drain the dal mixture and transfer to a large saucepan, along with 750 ml (25½ fl oz/3 cups) water and the spice bundle. Bring to the boil over high heat, skimming off any froth that rises to the surface. Reduce the heat to low and simmer, stirring occasionally, for about 1½ hours, until the dal is tender. Add a little more boiling water if the mixture starts to stick to the bottom of the pan or is becoming too thick.

Remove and discard the spice bundle. Add the tomatoes, butter, ginger, garlic, chilli powder, turmeric and a good pinch of salt. Increase the heat to medium and cook, stirring frequently, for 10 minutes. The consistency should be like a thick soup. Taste, and adjust the seasoning if necessary. Stir in the fenugreek leaves.

Serve with steamed basmati rice or puri, if you like.

2 tablespoons ghee or peanut
    (ground nut) oil

1 teaspoon cumin seeds

1 onion, chopped

2 garlic cloves, crushed

2 cm (¾ in) piece ginger, finely grated

1 small red chilli, chopped

1½ teaspoons sweet paprika

1 teaspoon ground coriander

¼ teaspoon ground turmeric

2 large tomatoes, finely chopped

2 x 400 g (14 oz) tins chickpeas (garbanzo
    beans), drained

1 teaspoon Garam masala (see page 218
    or use store-bought)

freshly squeezed lemon juice, to taste plus
    extra wedges, to serve

coriander (cilantro) leaves, to serve

steamed basmati rice (see page 178)
    or your favourite Indian flatbreads,
    to serve

SERVES 4

Chana masala
India

Heat the ghee or oil in a medium saucepan over medium heat. Add the cumin seeds and allow to sizzle for 10 seconds, then add the onion and cook, stirring occasionally, for 5–6 minutes, until starting to brown. Add the garlic, ginger and chilli and cook for 1 minute until fragrant. Add the paprika, coriander and turmeric and cook, stirring, for 2 minutes, or until fragrant. Add the tomato and stir for 1 minute, then add 250 ml (8½ fl oz/1 cup) water and a good pinch of salt. Bring to the boil, cover, then reduce the heat and simmer for 10 minutes for the flavours to develop.

Add the chickpeas, then bring to the boil again. Reduce the heat, cover and simmer, stirring occasionally, for 20 minutes. Remove the lid and simmer for a further 10–15 minutes, until the sauce is thickened and the spices have mellowed. Add a little more boiling water if the mixture starts to stick to the bottom of the pan or is becoming too thick. Remove from the heat and stir in the garam masala and lemon juice to taste. Taste and adjust the seasoning if necessary.

Serve with steamed basmati rice or flatbreads and lemon wedges for squeezing over.

Masoor dal
Bangladesh

200 g (7 oz/1 cup) masoor dal (split
    red lentils), well rinsed
1 onion, chopped
2 fresh or dried bay leaves
    (preferably Indian)
½ teaspoon ground cumin
½ teaspoon ground turmeric
¼ teaspoon freshly ground black pepper
1 teaspoon salt
1 tablespoon vegetable oil
3 small tomatoes, cut into wedges
1 floury potato, peeled and chopped
large handful coriander (cilantro), chopped
steamed basmati rice (see page 178),
    to serve
lemon wedges, to serve (optional)

Temper
3 tablespoons ghee
½ teaspoon cumin seeds
½ teaspoon black mustard seeds
½ teaspoon fennel seeds
2 small dried red chillies
1 small onion, thinly sliced
2 long green chillies, sliced
3 cm (1¼ in) piece ginger, julienned
2 garlic cloves, sliced

SERVES 4

Combine the masoor dal, onion, bay leaves, spices, salt, oil and 750 ml (25¼ fl oz/3 cups) water in a large heavy-based saucepan. Place over medium heat and bring to the boil. Add the tomato and potato, then reduce the heat to low and simmer, stirring occasionally, for 25–30 minutes, until the lentils and potato are soft and broken down. Add a little more boiling water if the mixture starts to stick to the bottom of the pan or is becoming too thick. The finished dal should be fairly thin and creamy, but not soupy.

To make the temper, heat the ghee in a frying pan over medium heat. Add the spices and dried chillies and sizzle for a few seconds, then add the onion, fresh chilli, ginger and garlic and cook, stirring occasionally, for 8–10 minutes, until golden.

Stir the temper into the cooked dal and cook for another 1–2 minutes. Stir in the coriander and season to taste.

Serve with steamed basmati rice and lemon wedges for squeezing over, if you like.

Moong dal

210 g (7½ oz/1 cup) moong dal (skinned split mung beans), well rinsed

¼ teaspoon ground turmeric

steamed basmati rice (see page 178) or Roti canai (see page 199), to serve

Temper

2 tablespoons ghee or peanut (ground nut) oil

1–2 whole dried red chillies

½ teaspoon cumin seeds

½ teaspoon fenugreek seeds

⅛ teaspoon asafoetida

1 Asian shallot, thinly sliced

1 sprig fresh curry leaves

SERVES 4–6

Place the moong dal in a medium saucepan and add 800 ml (27 fl oz) water. Bring to the boil over high heat and skim off the froth that rises to the surface. Stir in the turmeric, then reduce the heat to medium–low, cover, leaving the lid open a crack, and simmer, stirring occasionally, for 35–40 minutes, until the moong dal is soft and broken down. Add a little more boiling water if the mixture starts to stick to the bottom of the pan or is becoming too thick. Add salt to taste. Remove from the heat and set aside.

To make the temper, heat the ghee or oil in a heavy-based frying pan over medium–high heat. Add the chilli, cumin, fenugreek and asafoetida. Shake the pan for about 30 seconds and as soon as the chillies start to darken, add the shallot and curry leaves. Cook, stirring, for 2–3 minutes, until the shallot starts to brown.

Give the dal a stir and thin with a little boiling water if necessary. Pour into a serving dish, top with the temper and stir until just combined.

Serve with steamed basmati rice or roti.

Doubles
Trinidad & Tobago

To make the bara, combine the flour, yeast, curry powder, cumin, white pepper and salt in a large bowl. Add 125 ml (4 fl oz/½ cup) warm water and the vegetable oil and mix to form a soft dough. Add a little more water if necessary. Cover and set aside for 20 minutes.

Turn the dough onto a floured work surface and knead for 1–2 minutes, until quite smooth. Cover and set aside in a warm place for 2–3 hours, until nearly doubled in size.

Meanwhile, to make the curried channa, heat the ghee or oil in a medium saucepan over medium heat. Add the onion and cook, stirring occasionally, for 5–6 minutes, until soft. Add the garlic and cook for 1 minute, until fragrant. Add the curry powder, cumin and allspice and cook, stirring, for 2 minutes, or until fragrant. Add the chilli, chickpeas, 250 ml (8½ fl oz/1 cup) water and a good pinch of salt. Bring to the boil, then reduce the heat to low and simmer for 20–25 minutes, until the sauce is slightly thickened. Add a little more boiling water if the mixture starts to stick to the bottom of the pan. Stir in the parsley and season to taste. Keep warm.

Lightly oil your fingers and divide the dough into 16 walnut-sized balls. On a lightly oiled work surface, flatten and gently stretch the balls of dough into 10 cm (4 in) rounds.

Heat enough oil for deep-frying in a deep-fryer or deep frying pan (no more than one-third full) over medium–high heat to 180°C (350°F) or until a small piece of dough dropped into the oil browns in 15 seconds. Working in batches, fry the bara for 15–30 seconds each side, until puffed and golden. Drain on paper towel.

Spoon the curried channa onto half the bara and top with the remaining bara.

Serve with hot pepper sauce and green mango pickle on the side.

Trinidadian Scotch bonnet pepper sauce (or other hot sauce), to serve
green mango pickle, to serve

Bara

225 g (8 oz/1½ cups) plain (all-purpose) flour, plus extra for dusting
1 teaspoons dried instant yeast
1 teaspoon curry powder (preferably Trinidadian, but all-purpose is fine)
½ teaspoon ground cumin
½ teaspoon ground white pepper
½ teaspoon salt
1 tablespoon vegetable oil, plus extra for greasing
peanut (ground nut) or vegetable oil, for deep-frying

Curried channa

1 tablespoon ghee or vegetable oil
1 onion, chopped
2 garlic cloves, crushed
1 tablespoon curry powder (preferably Trinidadian, but all-purpose is fine)
2 teaspoons ground cumin
½ teaspoon ground allspice
1 Scotch bonnet or habanero chilli, pricked all over with the tip of a knife
400 g (14 oz) tin chickpeas (garbanzo beans), drained
small handful flat-leaf parsley, roughly chopped

SERVES 4

Chana dal
India

200 g (7 oz/1 cup) chana dal (split
    chickpeas/yellow split peas), well rinsed
1½ teaspoons ground turmeric
½ teaspoon ground cardamom
1 fresh or dried bay leaf (preferably Indian)
½ teaspoon Garam masala (see page 218
    or use store-bought)
freshly squeezed lemon juice, to taste
coriander (cilantro) leaves, roughly
    chopped, to serve
steamed basmati rice (see page 178),
    to serve

Temper

2 tablespoons ghee or sunflower oil
6 whole cloves
½ teaspoon black mustard seeds
2 dried red chillies, cracked open
pinch of asafoetida
4 garlic cloves, crushed
½ teaspoon cumin seeds

SERVES 4

Combine the chana dal, turmeric, cardamom, bay leaf and 1 litre (34 fl oz/4 cups) water in a large heavy-based saucepan over medium heat and bring to the boil. Reduce the heat to a low simmer, cover, leaving the lid open a crack and cook, stirring occasionally, for 50–60 minutes, until the chana dal is soft and broken down (see note). Add a little more boiling water if the mixture starts to stick to the bottom of the pan or is becoming too thick. Remove and discard the bay leaf and season generously with salt. Purée with a stick blender if you prefer a smoother dal.

To make the temper, heat the ghee or oil in a small saucepan over medium–high heat. Add the cloves, mustard seeds and chilli and cook, shaking the pan, until the seeds start to crackle. Add the asafoetida, garlic and cumin seeds and cook, stirring constantly, for 30 seconds or until fragrant.

Pour the temper over the dal and add the garam masala. Stir gently to combine. Taste and season with a little more salt if needed and a good squeeze of lemon juice.

Scatter with coriander and serve with steamed basmati rice.

NOTE: YOU CAN REDUCE THE COOKING TIME OF THE DAL BY SOAKING THE CHANA DAL IN COLD WATER PRIOR TO COOKING FOR 2–3 HOURS. DRAIN AND FOLLOW THE RECIPE, REDUCING THE COOKING TIME TO ABOUT 30 MINUTES.

2 medium tomatoes

3 tablespoons pure peanut butter

400 ml (14 fl oz) tin coconut milk

50 g (1¾ oz) butter or ghee

1 large onion, finely chopped

1 tablespoon all-purpose curry powder

1.2 kg (2 lb 10 oz) English spinach, washed very well, leaves removed, roughly chopped

½–1 teaspoon salt, to taste

steamed rice, to serve

SERVES 4

Mchicha
Tanzania

Place the tomatoes in a heatproof bowl and cover with boiling water. Set aside for 1–2 minutes, then drain. When cool enough to handle, gently peel the skins and discard. Finely chop the flesh.

Whisk the peanut butter and coconut milk in a small bowl or jug.

Melt the butter or ghee in a large frying pan over low heat. Add the onion and cook for 10 minutes, until soft. Increase the heat to medium and add the curry powder. Stir for 2 minutes, then add the tomato and cook for a further 3–4 minutes.

Add the spinach and cook over medium heat for 10 minutes, or until the spinach is wilted and cooked down. Add the coconut milk and peanut butter and simmer for a further 5 minutes, or until heated through. Season to taste with salt.

Serve with steamed rice.

Misir wat
Ethiopia

50 g (1¾ oz) Nit'r kibbeh (see page 104) or ghee

1 onion, finely chopped

3 garlic cloves, crushed

2 tablespoons tomato paste (concentrated purée)

200 g (7 oz/1 cup) masoor dal (split red lentils), well rinsed

1 tablespoon Berbere spice mix (see page 219), plus extra to taste

1 tomato, chopped

Injera (see page 193), to serve

SERVES 4

Heat the nit'r kibbeh or ghee in a medium saucepan over medium heat. Add the onion and cook, stirring occasionally, for 8–10 minutes, until golden brown. Add the garlic and cook, stirring constantly, for about 30 seconds, until fragrant. Add the tomato paste and cook, stirring constantly, for 2 minutes. Add the masoor dal, berbere spice mix, tomato and 750 ml (25½ fl oz/3 cups) water and bring to the boil. Reduce the heat to medium–low and simmer, stirring occasionally, for 25–30 minutes, until the lentils are tender and the mixture is fairly thick. Add a little more boiling water if the mixture starts to stick to the bottom of the pan. Stir in a little more berbere to taste, if you like and season if necessary.

Serve with injera.

Cashew curry
Sri Lanka

300 g (10½ oz/2 cups) cashew nuts
2 tablespoons melted coconut oil
1 sprig curry leaves
1 onion, chopped
2 long green chillies, thinly sliced
20 cm (8 in) length pandan leaf, tied
   in a knot
2 garlic cloves, thinly sliced
2 cm (¾ in) piece ginger, finely grated
½ teaspoon ground cumin
½ teaspoon ground turmeric
½ teaspoon cayenne pepper
400 ml (13½ fl oz) tin coconut milk
200 g (7 oz) snake (yard-long) beans, cut
   into 4 cm (1½ in) lengths
½ teaspoon Garam masala (see page 218
   or use store-bought)
steamed basmati rice (see page 178),
   to serve

SERVES 4

Place the cashew nuts in a bowl and cover with cold water. Set aside for 1 hour to soften slightly. Drain and discard the water.

Heat the coconut oil in a large frying pan with a lid over medium heat. Add the curry leaves and sizzle for a few seconds, then add the onion, chilli, pandan leaf, garlic and ginger. Cook, stirring occasionally, for 4–5 minutes, until the onion starts to brown. Add the cumin, turmeric and cayenne pepper and cook, stirring, for 1 minute, until fragrant.

Add the cashew nuts to the pan, along with the coconut milk, 125 ml (4 fl oz/½ cup) water and a generous pinch of salt. Mix well and bring to the boil. Reduce the heat to a simmer, cover and cook, stirring occasionally, for 30 minutes, until the sauce has thickened slightly. Simmer, uncovered, for a few more minutes if the mixture is very runny.

Add the snake beans and cook, covered, for 10 minutes, or until the beans are tender. Stir in the garam masala.

Serve with steamed basmati rice.

Dal bhat
Nepal

200 g (7 oz/1 cup) masoor dal (split
　　red lentils), well rinsed
½ teaspoon salt
2 tablespoons ghee
1 onion, chopped
½ teaspoon ground coriander
½ teaspoon ground cumin
½ teaspoon chilli powder
½ teaspoon ground turmeric
¼ teaspoon ground cardamom
¼ teaspoon ground cinnamon
pinch of ground cloves
Vegetable tarkari (see page 36), to serve
stir-fried mustard greens, to serve

SERVES 4

Combine the masoor dal and salt with 375 ml (12½ fl oz/1½ cups) water in a medium saucepan over medium heat and bring to the boil. Reduce the heat to a low simmer, then cover, leaving the lid open a crack, and cook, stirring occasionally, for 20–25 minutes, until the lentils are soft and broken down. Add a little more boiling water if the mixture starts to stick to the bottom of the pan or is becoming too thick – the finished dal should be quite soupy.

Meanwhile, heat the ghee in a small frying pan over medium heat. Add the onion and cook, stirring occasionally, for 8–10 minutes, until golden. Add the spices and cook for 2–3 minutes, until fragrant. Stir the spice mixture into the dal.

Serve with vegetable tarkari and stir-fried mustard greens.

MALAI KOFTA

32

EGGPLANT MASALA

35

VEGETABLE TARKARI

36

CARIBBEAN PLANTAIN CURRY

38

SAAG ALOO

40

VEGETABLE YELLOW CURRY

41

BEETROOT CURRY

42

GOLDEN EGG CURRY

45

SAAG PANEER

46

OKRA CURRY

48

POTATO CURRY

49

VEGETABLE JUNGLE CURRY

50

CHIP SHOP CURRY SAUCE & CHIPS

52

Vegetables

Malai kofta
India

To make the kofta, place the potatoes in a saucepan, cover with cold water and add a good pinch of salt. Bring to the boil and cook until tender. Drain, then mash and set aside to cool a little.

Combine the potato, paneer, cashew nuts, raisins, cornflour, garam masala, salt and chilli powder in a medium bowl. Knead the mixture until you have a soft dough, then divide into 12 portions and roll into smooth balls. Set aside.

To make the sauce, heat three-quarters of the oil in a deep frying pan over low heat. Add the onion, garlic and ginger and cook, stirring occasionally, for 10 minutes, or until the onion is soft. Add the tomato, cashew nuts and 250 ml (8½ fl oz/1 cup) water and simmer for 5–7 minutes, until slightly thickened. Season to taste with salt. Transfer the mixture to a food processor or use a stick blender to blitz to a smooth sauce. Wipe the pan clean.

Heat the remaining oil in the same pan over medium heat and add the cumin seeds, coriander, turmeric, bay leaf, cinnamon stick, cloves and cardamom pods and cook, stirring, for 1 minute, until fragrant. Pour the sauce back into the pan and add the fenugreek leaves and garam masala. Gently warm through.

Heat the vegetable oil in a wok or deep frying pan to 190° (375°F) or until a breadcrumb dropped into the oil turns brown in 15 seconds. Working in batches, add the kofta and deep-fry for 2–3 minutes, moving them around with a metal slotted spoon, until well browned on all sides. Remove the kofta to a plate lined with paper towel to drain.

Dip each kofta into the cream and add to the sauce to warm through. Sprinkle over the coriander leaves, if using.

Serve the malai kofta in their sauce with steamed basmati rice and naan on the side.

60 ml (2 fl oz/¼ cup) cream

coriander (cilantro) leaves, to serve (optional)

steamed basmati rice (see page 178), to serve

Simple naan (see page 194), to serve

Kofta

2 medium (about 400 g/14 oz) floury potatoes, peeled

100 g (3½ oz/1 cup) grated paneer cheese

1 tablespoon finely chopped cashew nuts

1 tablespoon finely chopped raisins

3 tablespoons cornflour (corn starch)

½ teaspoon Garam masala (see page 218 or use store-bought)

½ teaspoon salt

½ teaspoon chilli powder (optional)

vegetable oil, for frying

Sauce

80 ml (2½ fl oz/⅓ cup) vegetable oil

1 medium onion, finely chopped

2 garlic cloves, crushed

3 cm (1¼ in) piece ginger, finely grated

500 ml (17 fl oz/2 cups) puréed tomatoes or 500 g (1 lb 2 oz) ripe tomatoes, chopped

2 tablespoons cashew nuts, finely ground

1 teaspoon cumin seeds

1 teaspoon ground coriander

½ teaspoon ground turmeric

1 fresh or dried bay leaf (preferably Indian)

1 cinnamon stick

4 whole cloves

3 green cardamom pods, bruised

1 black cardamom pod, bruised (optional)

½ teaspoon dried fenugreek leaves

½ teaspoon Garam masala (see page 218 or use store-bought)

SERVES 4

2 large (about 900 g/2 lb) eggplants (aubergines), cut into 2 cm (¾ in) chunks

½ teaspoon salt

2 tablespoons ghee or vegetable oil

1 teaspoon black mustard seeds

3 Asian shallots, sliced

2 cm (¾ in) piece ginger, finely grated

2 garlic cloves, thinly sliced

1 long red chilli, chopped

400 g (14 oz) tin crushed tomatoes

½ teaspoon ground cinnamon

¼ teaspoon ground cardamom

pinch of ground cloves

60 g (2 oz/¼ cup) plain yoghurt

coriander (cilantro) leaves, to serve (optional)

papadums, to serve

SERVES 4

Eggplant masala

India

Place the eggplant in a large bowl and sprinkle with the salt. Toss to combine and set aside for 30 minutes. Rinse well and pat dry with paper towel.

Heat a large heavy-based frying pan over high heat. Working in batches if necessary, add the eggplant to the dry pan and cook, stirring occasionally, for 5–6 minutes per batch, until lightly browned all over. Transfer to a plate and set aside.

Heat the ghee or oil in the same frying pan over medium–high heat. Add the mustard seeds and sizzle for a few seconds. When the seeds start to crackle, add the shallot, ginger, garlic and chilli. Reduce the heat to medium and cook for 4–5 minutes, stirring occasionally, until the onion is golden. Add the tomato, cinnamon, cardamom, cloves and 125 ml (4 fl oz/½ cup) water and return the eggplant to the pan. Cover and cook, stirring occasionally, for 10–15 minutes, until the eggplant is very tender and the sauce has thickened slightly. Season with a little salt, if necessary.

Spoon the yoghurt over the curry, scatter with coriander leaves, if using, and serve with papadums on the side.

Vegetable tarkari
Nepal

2 tablespoons ghee

2 onions, chopped

1–2 long green chillies, to taste

1 fresh or dried bay leaf

3 garlic cloves, crushed

2.5 cm (1 in) piece ginger, finely grated

2 teaspoons cumin seeds

1 teaspoon coriander seeds

¼ teaspoon ground turmeric

sea salt

2 potatoes, cut into 1.5 cm (½ in) pieces

½ cauliflower, cut into small florets

3 tomatoes, quartered

120 g (4½ oz/1 cup) fresh soybeans (edamame)

freshly ground black pepper

coriander (cilantro) leaves, to serve (optional)

steamed basmati rice (see page 178), to serve

Dal bhat, to serve (see page 29)

SERVES 4

Heat the ghee in a large saucepan over medium–low heat. Add the onion and cook, stirring occasionally, for 8–10 minutes, until golden. Add the chilli, bay leaf, garlic, ginger and spices, along with a good pinch of sea salt and cook for 1–2 minutes, until fragrant. Add the potato and cook, stirring occasionally, for 4–5 minutes, until the potato starts to brown. Add the cauliflower, tomato and 250 ml (8½ fl oz/1 cup) water. Bring to the boil, then reduce the heat and simmer for 10 minutes. Add the soybeans and cook for a further 5 minutes, or until the vegetables are tender. Taste and season generously with freshly ground black pepper and a little more salt if necessary.

Scatter the curry with coriander leaves, if using, and serve with steamed basmati rice and dal bhat on the side.

Caribbean plantain curry

Jamaica

2 tablespoons coconut or vegetable oil

1 leek, white part only, sliced

3 garlic cloves, crushed

3 cm (1¼ in) piece ginger, finely grated

1 tablespoon Jamaican curry powder
(or all-purpose curry powder)

1 teaspoon ground turmeric

1 teaspoon ground allspice

½ teaspoon ground white pepper

½ teaspoon salt

3 green plantains, peeled and cut into 1 cm
(½ in) thick diagonal slices

4 fresh thyme sprigs

1–2 scotch bonnet, habanero or other hot
chillies, pricked all over with the tip of
a knife

270 ml (9 fl oz) tin coconut milk

250 ml (8½ fl oz/1 cup) vegetable stock

400 g (14 oz) tin black-eyed peas, rinsed
and drained

juice of ½ lime, to taste

sliced spring onions (scallions), to serve

steamed rice or flatbreads, to serve

SERVES 4

Heat the oil in a medium heavy-based saucepan over medium–low heat. Add the leek and cook, stirring, for 6–8 minutes, until softened. Add the garlic and ginger and cook for 2 minutes, then sprinkle in the curry powder, spices and salt and cook, stirring, for 2 minutes, or until fragrant.

Add the plantain, thyme and chillies. Pour in the coconut milk and stock, adding a little extra water if necessary to just cover the plantains. Increase the heat to high and bring to the boil, then reduce the heat and simmer, uncovered and stirring occasionally, for 25–30 minutes, until the plantain starts to soften. Stir in the peas and simmer for a further 5–10 minutes until cooked through. Add the lime juice to taste and season if necessary.

Scatter the curry with spring onion and serve with steamed rice or flatbreads.

Saag aloo
India

3 tablespoons ghee
1 teaspoon black mustard seeds
1 onion, chopped
3 garlic cloves, thinly sliced
3 cm (1¼ in) piece ginger, finely grated
1 teaspoon cumin seeds
1 teaspoon ground turmeric
½ teaspoon chilli powder
600 g (1 lb 5 oz) waxy or all-purpose
    potatoes, scrubbed and chopped into
    1.5 cm (½ in) pieces
200 g (7 oz) baby spinach leaves
squeeze of lemon juice, to taste (optional)

SERVES 4–6 AS PART OF A SHARED MEAL

Heat 1 tablespoon of the ghee in a large non-stick frying pan over medium heat and add the mustard seeds. Let the seeds sizzle for a few seconds, until they start to crackle. Add the onion, garlic, ginger and spices and cook, stirring, for 4–5 minutes, until the onion is deep golden. Transfer to a plate with a slotted spoon.

Add the remaining ghee, the potato and a generous pinch of salt to the same frying pan. Stir to coat the potato in the ghee and add 80 ml (2½ fl oz/⅓ cup) water. Cover, and cook for 5 minutes or until the potato starts to soften. Remove the lid and cook for a further 10–15 minutes, letting the potato cook undisturbed for periods of time so that a nice crust forms.

Return the onion mixture to the pan and add the spinach, turning gently until wilted. Season to taste and add a little lemon juice if you like.

Serve as part of a shared meal with your choice of rice, breads and other curries.

Vegetable yellow curry
Thailand

2 tablespoons peanut (ground nut) oil

300 g (10½ oz) firm tofu, cut into 2 cm (¾ in) cubes

2 teaspoons ground turmeric

270 ml (9 fl oz) tin coconut milk (do not shake before opening)

1 large red onion, cut into thin wedges

3 tablespoons Yellow curry paste (see page 208)

500 ml (17 fl oz/2 cups) vegetable stock

250 g (9 oz) pumpkin (winter squash), peeled, seeded and chopped into 4 cm (1½ in) pieces

2 carrots, cut diagonally into chunks

1 tablespoon fish sauce, plus extra to taste

2 teaspoons grated palm sugar, plus extra to taste

200 g (7 oz) cauliflower, cut into florets

200 g (7 oz) snake (yard-long) beans, cut into 5 cm (2 in) lengths

200 g (7 oz) peeled and sliced lotus root (see note)

100 g (3½ oz) snow peas (mangetout), trimmed and cut diagonally in half

1 tablespoon freshly squeezed lime juice, plus extra to taste

steamed brown rice or quinoa, to serve

unsalted roasted cashew nuts, to serve

coriander (cilantro) leaves, to serve

SERVES 4

NOTE: LOTUS ROOT CAN BE FOUND EITHER FRESH OR FROZEN FROM ASIAN GROCERS. ALTERNATIVELY SUBSTITUTE WATER CHESTNUTS OR DAIKON (WHITE RADISH) IF UNAVAILABLE.

THIS CURRY IS ALSO GREAT MADE WITH GREEN CURRY PASTE (SEE PAGE 207).

Heat the oil in a large heavy-based saucepan over medium–low heat. Add the tofu and turmeric and cook, carefully turning the tofu, for 4–5 minutes, until the tofu is well coated in the turmeric and lightly browned. Transfer to a plate and set aside.

Add 2 tablespoons of the cream from the top of the coconut milk tin and the onion to the saucepan and cook, stirring occasionally, for 2–3 minutes, until the onion is just tender. Add the curry paste and cook, stirring, for 1–2 minutes, until fragrant.

Add a little of the stock to the pan and stir to deglaze and loosen any paste stuck to the bottom. Add the pumpkin, carrot, the remaining stock, fish sauce and sugar, and bring to the boil. Reduce the heat to low and simmer, covered, for 4 minutes. Stir in the cauliflower and snake beans, then cover and cook for 8 minutes. Stir in the lotus root, snow peas, remaining coconut milk and lime juice and return the tofu to the pan. Cook for 5 minutes or until heated through and all the vegetables are tender. Season to taste with extra fish sauce, lime juice and palm sugar to balance the flavour if necessary.

Serve with steamed brown rice or quinoa and scattered with cashew nuts and coriander.

Beetroot curry
Sri Lanka

3 tablespoons ghee
1 large onion, thinly sliced
1 long green chilli, sliced
20 cm (8 in) length pandan leaf, tied
    in a knot
1 sprig curry leaves
2 garlic cloves, thinly sliced
1 tomato, chopped
2 (about 350 g/12½ oz) beetroot (beets),
    peeled and cut into thick batons
1 cinnamon stick
1 teaspoon ground coriander
1 teaspoon Kashmiri chilli powder
½ teaspoon ground turmeric
1 tablespoon white vinegar
300 ml (10½ fl oz) coconut milk
steamed basmati rice (see page 178),
    to serve

SERVES 4

Heat the ghee in a heavy-based saucepan over medium heat. Add the onion and green chilli and cook, stirring occasionally, for 6–8 minutes, until softened. Add the pandan leaf, curry leaves and garlic, and cook for a further 3 minutes, or until fragrant. Add the tomato and cook for 2–3 minutes, until it starts to break down.

Add the remaining ingredients to the pan and give everything a good stir. Cover and simmer over very low heat, stirring occasionally, for 15–20 minutes, until the beetroot is tender. Add a little water to thin the sauce if necessary and season to taste.

Serve with steamed basmati rice.

Golden egg curry

Myanmar

3 tablespoons peanut (ground nut) oil, plus extra to shallow-fry

1 red onion, thinly sliced

1 teaspoon ground turmeric

5 tomatoes, halved

3 garlic cloves, crushed

2 cm (¾ in) piece ginger, finely grated

3 long green chillies, thinly sliced

1 teaspoon chilli powder

1 tablespoon fish sauce, or to taste

4 large free-range eggs, at room temperature

coriander (cilantro) leaves, to serve (optional)

steamed rice, to serve

SERVES 4

NOTE: COOKING THE EGGS FOR 6 MINUTES WILL GIVE YOU SOFT AND JAMMY CENTRES. COOK THE EGGS FOR A FURTHER 1–2 MINUTES, IF YOU PREFER FIRM YOLKS.

Heat the 3 tablespoons of oil in a medium heavy-based frying pan over medium heat. Add the onion and half the turmeric and cook, stirring occasionally, for 5–6 minutes, until golden.

Meanwhile, grate the tomato using a box grater resting on a plate to catch all the juices. Discard the skin left behind.

Stir the garlic and ginger into the onion and cook, stirring, for 1–2 minutes, until fragrant. Increase the heat to medium–high, add the tomato pulp and juice, half the sliced chillies and the chilli powder and cook, stirring often, for 10–12 minutes, until the mixture is slightly thickened. Stir in the fish sauce and a generous grinding of black pepper, taste and add a little more if necessary.

Meanwhile, gently lower the eggs into a small saucepan of boiling water. Reduce the heat to medium–low and cook for 6 minutes (see note). Drain the eggs and run them under cold water until cool enough to handle. Gently peel and pat the eggs dry with paper towel.

Heat enough oil for shallow-frying in a small saucepan over medium–high heat. Add the remaining turmeric and stir to dissolve. Carefully add the peeled eggs and fry, turning the eggs regularly and basting with the hot oil, for 2–3 minutes, until golden.

Reheat the tomato mixture if necessary, then cut the eggs in half and nestle them in the sauce.

To serve, scatter the coriander, if using, and remaining sliced chilli over the eggs in their curry sauce and serve with steamed rice.

Saag paneer
India

2 tablespoons ghee

300 g (10½ oz) paneer cheese, cut into 1.5 cm (½ in) cubes

½ teaspoon black mustard seeds

1 onion, thinly sliced

3 garlic cloves, thinly sliced

2 cm (¾ in) piece ginger, julienned

½ teaspoon chilli powder

½ teaspoon ground turmeric

500 g (1 lb 2 oz) English spinach, washed and tough stalks removed, leaves roughly shredded

¼ teaspoon Garam masala (see page 218 or use store-bought)

squeeze of lemon juice, to taste (optional)

SERVES 4–6 AS PART OF A SHARED MEAL

Heat 1 tablespoon of the ghee in a large non-stick frying pan over medium–high heat. Working in batches if necessary, add the paneer and fry for 5–6 minutes, turning so that at least 2–3 sides are well browned. Transfer the paneer to a plate with a slotted spoon and sprinkle lightly with salt.

Heat the remaining ghee in the same frying pan over medium–high heat. Add the mustard seeds and let them sizzle for a few seconds, until they start to crackle. Add the onion, garlic, ginger, chilli and turmeric to the pan and cook, stirring, for 4–5 minutes, until the onion is well coloured.

Add the shredded spinach (in batches if necessary, so that it all fits in the pan), turning constantly with a pair of tongs until wilted. Return the paneer to the pan and stir until hot. Stir in the garam masala, season to taste and add a little lemon juice if you like.

Serve as part of a shared meal with your choice of rice, breads and other curries.

Okra curry
India

125 ml (4 fl oz/½ cup) vegetable or peanut (ground nut) oil

500 g (1 lb 2 oz) okra, ends trimmed

1 large onion, finely chopped

4 garlic cloves, finely chopped

3 cm (1¼ in) piece ginger, finely grated

2 teaspoons ground cumin

2 teaspoons ground coriander

1 teaspoon chilli powder

½ teaspoon ground turmeric

4 large tomatoes, roughly chopped

½ teaspoon salt

1 teaspoon Garam masala (see page 218 or use store-bought)

small handful chopped coriander (cilantro)

¼–½ teaspoon amchur powder (dried green mango powder) (optional)

Chapattis (see page 190), Simple naan (see page 194) or steamed basmati rice (see page 178), to serve

SERVES 4

Heat 2 tablespoons of the oil in a large deep frying pan over medium–high heat. Add half the okra and cook, stirring occasionally, for 10 minutes, until golden and slightly shrivelled. Remove to a plate. Repeat with another 2 tablespoons of the oil and the remaining okra, then add this okra to the cooked batch.

In the same pan, heat the remaining oil over medium heat. Add the onion and cook for 5–8 minutes, until soft. Add the garlic, ginger and spices and cook, stirring, for 2 minutes, until fragrant. Add the tomato, salt, fried okra and 125 ml (4 fl oz/½ cup) water and cook, covered, for 5 minutes, or until the okra is very soft. Stir in the garam masala, coriander and amchur powder and season with salt, to taste.

Serve with chapattis, naan, or steamed basmati rice.

3 tablespoons vegetable oil or ghee

1 teaspoon black mustard seeds

½ teaspoon cumin seeds

1 sprig curry leaves

1 onion, chopped

2 tomatoes, chopped

1 long green chilli, sliced, plus extra
    to serve

2 teaspoons ground coriander

2 teaspoons Kashmiri chilli powder

½ teaspoon ground turmeric

600 g (1 lb 5 oz) waxy potatoes, scrubbed
    and chopped into 2 cm (¾ in) pieces

1 teaspoon salt

125 ml (4 fl oz/½ cup) coconut milk

large handful coriander (cilantro) leaves,
    roughly chopped, plus extra to serve

1 teaspoon dried fenugreek leaves

steamed basmati rice (see page 178) or
    Paratha (see page 191), to serve

SERVES 4–6

Potato curry
India

Heat the oil or ghee in a large non-stick saucepan over medium–high heat. Add the mustard seeds, cumin seeds and curry leaves and sizzle for a few seconds, until they start to crackle. Add the onion, then reduce the heat to medium and cook, stirring, for about 3 minutes, or until the onion has softened.

Add the tomato, green chilli and spices and cook, stirring, for 2–3 minutes, until the tomato begins to break down. Add the potato, salt and 250 ml (8½ fl oz/1 cup) water. Bring to the boil, then reduce the heat and simmer, covered, for 15–20 minutes, until the potato is tender.

Add the coconut milk, stir well and bring the mixture back to a simmer. Remove from the heat and stir in the coriander and fenugreek leaves.

Serve, topped with the extra chilli and coriander and with steamed basmati rice or paratha on the side.

Vegetable jungle curry
Thailand

60 ml (2 fl oz/¼ cup) vegetable or peanut (ground nut) oil

80 g (2½ oz/⅓ cup) Jungle curry paste (see page 210)

3 garlic cloves, crushed

2 cm (¾ in) piece ginger, finely grated

100 g (3½ oz) baby corn, halved

100 g (3½ oz) pea eggplants (aubergines), quartered

100 g (3½ oz) snake (yard-long) beans, cut into 3 cm (1¼ in) lengths

100 g (3½ oz) tomatoes, cut into wedges

150 g (5 oz) firm tofu, cut into 2.5 cm (1 in) cubes

3 green bird's eye chillies, halved

2 tablespoons fish sauce, or to taste

2 tablespoons sugar, or to taste

2 tablespoons freshly squeezed lime juice, or to taste

Thai basil or coriander (cilantro) leaves, to serve (optional)

thinly sliced red onion, to serve

steamed jasmine rice (see page 178), to serve

SERVES 4

Heat the oil in a large deep frying pan or wok. Add the curry paste, garlic and ginger and cook, stirring, for 2–3 minutes until fragrant. Add 625 ml (21 fl oz/2½ cups) water and bring to a simmer. Add the vegetables, tofu and green chillies and simmer for 3–5 minutes, until the vegetables are just tender. Season to taste with the fish sauce, sugar, lime juice and a pinch of salt. The flavour should be hot, salty and sour.

Scatter the herbs, if using, and red onion over the top of the curry and serve with jasmine rice on the side.

Chip shop curry sauce & chips

U.K.

1 tablespoon butter

1 tablespoon peanut (ground nut) oil

2 onions, finely chopped

2 garlic cloves, crushed

1 tablespoon tomato paste (concentrated purée)

2 tablespoons plain (all-purpose) flour

1 tablespoon all-purpose curry powder, or to taste (use a hot curry powder if you prefer a spicier curry sauce)

1 teaspoon sweet paprika

375 ml (12½ fl oz/1½ cups) chicken or vegetable stock

½ teaspoon soy sauce

squeeze of lemon juice, to taste

hot chips (fries) and vinegar, to serve

SERVES 4

Heat the butter and oil in a medium saucepan over low heat. Add the onion and garlic and cook, stirring frequently, for 6–8 minutes, until softened. Add the tomato paste and cook, stirring, for 1 minute, then stir in the flour, curry powder and paprika. Cook, stirring constantly, for 1–2 minutes, until the mixture starts to stick on the base of the pan. Remove the pan from the heat and gradually whisk in the stock until smooth. Return the pan to medium heat, bring to the boil, stirring often, then reduce the heat to low and simmer, stirring occasionally, for 8–10 minutes, until thickened.

Blitz with a hand-held blender for a smooth sauce or just blend it a little, to leave some texture. Stir in the soy sauce, a squeeze of lemon juice to taste and add a little salt if necessary. Add a little boiling water to thin the consistency if you prefer a thinner sauce.

To serve, sprinkle the hot chips generously with vinegar and spoon over the sauce.

Best eaten late at night after a few drinks.

Seafood

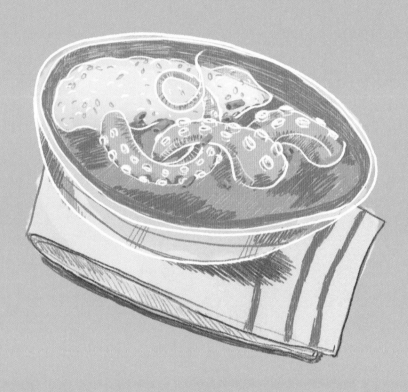

100 g (3½ oz) dried rice vermicelli

60 ml (2 fl oz/¼ cup) vegetable oil

1 x quantity Laksa paste (see page 214)

2 teaspoons grated palm sugar, plus extra to taste

1.5 litres (51 fl oz/6 cups) chicken stock

12 large raw green king prawns (shrimp), peeled and deveined with tails left intact

500 ml (17 fl oz/2 cups) coconut milk

150 g (5½ oz) fish balls

150 g (5½ oz) tofu puffs, thickly sliced

200 g (7 oz) bean sprouts, trimmed

300 g (10½ oz) fresh egg (hokkien) noodles

1 small green cucumber, julienned

crispy fried shallots, to serve

Vietnamese mint leaves, to serve

lime wedges, to serve

SERVES 4

Prawn & tofu laksa
Malaysia

Place the rice vermicelli in a large heatproof bowl and pour over enough boiling water to cover. Stand for 10–15 minutes, until tender. Drain well.

Heat the oil in a large saucepan or wok over medium heat. Add the laksa paste and cook, stirring, for 2–3 minutes, until fragrant. Add the sugar and stock. Stir well and bring to the boil. Reduce the heat to a simmer and add the prawns. Cook for 1 minute, or until the prawns are almost cooked. Add the coconut milk, fish balls and tofu puffs. Stir gently to combine, then bring almost to a simmer. Reduce the heat to low and cook for 2 minutes, or until the prawns are just cooked and the fish balls and tofu are heated through. Stir in the bean sprouts.

Meanwhile, place the egg noodles in a large heatproof bowl. Pour over enough boiling water to cover, then stand for 2 minutes or until heated through. Drain well.

Divide both noodles among deep serving bowls and spoon over the laksa mixture, evenly dividing the prawns, fish balls, tofu puffs and bean sprouts among them. Top with the cucumber, crispy shallots and mint. Serve immediately with lime wedges for squeezing over.

Kerala-style fish curry

India

600 g (1 lb 5 oz) thick firm white fish
  fillets, cut into 3 cm (1¼ in) pieces
1 teaspoon ground turmeric
2 tablespoons melted coconut oil
1 sprig curry leaves
2 Asian shallots, sliced
3 cm (1¼ in) piece ginger, julienned
1 long red chilli, thinly sliced
½ teaspoon chilli powder
1 tablespoon sweet paprika
1–2 teaspoons tamarind purée, to taste
300 ml (10½ fl oz) tinned coconut milk
coriander (cilantro) leaves, to serve
steamed basmati rice (see page 178),
  to serve

SERVES 4

Sprinkle the fish with a little salt and ¼ teaspoon of the turmeric and toss gently to coat. Cover and set aside.

Heat the coconut oil in a large frying pan over medium–high heat. Add the curry leaves and sizzle for a few seconds, then add the shallot and cook, stirring occasionally, for 4–5 minutes, or until starting to brown. Add the ginger and sliced chilli and cook for 1 minute until fragrant. Add 250 ml (8½ fl oz/1 cup) water, the remaining turmeric, chilli powder, paprika and 1 teaspoon of the tamarind purée. Season generously with salt and freshly ground black pepper. Bring to a simmer, reduce the heat to low and simmer, stirring occasionally, for 5 minutes. Add the coconut milk and bring back to a simmer.

Add the fish to the sauce, stir gently and cook, spooning the sauce over the fish so that it cooks evenly, for 8–10 minutes, until just cooked through. Taste, and season with a little more tamarind purée to balance the flavour if necessary.

Scatter with coriander and serve with steamed basmati rice.

1.2 kg (2 lb 10 oz) mud or blue swimmer
    crabs, well cleaned

Green seasoning

2 spring onions (scallions), trimmed

2 garlic cloves, peeled

2 tablespoons coriander (cilantro) leaves

1 tablespoon thyme leaves

1 tablespoon parsley leaves

½ small banana pepper, or use 1 celery
    stalk if unavailable

Dumplings

300 g (10½ oz/2 cups) plain
    (all-purpose) flour

1 teaspoon salt

Curry

60 ml (2 fl oz/¼ cup) vegetable oil

1 white or brown onion, finely chopped

5 garlic cloves, crushed

2 mild pimento peppers, seeded
    and sliced

1 teaspoon cumin seeds

3 tablespoons Madras curry powder mixed
    with 80 ml (2½ fl oz/⅓ cup) water

1 teaspoon ground turmeric

500 ml (17 fl oz/2 cups) coconut milk

125 ml (4 fl oz/½ cup) fish stock or water

1 Scotch bonnet chilli, pricked all over
    with the tip of a knife

½ teaspoon sugar

squeeze of lime juice

coriander (cilantro) leaves, to serve

SERVES 4–6

Curried crab with dumplings
Trinidad & Tobago

If you've purchased live crabs, place them in the freezer for 1 hour, to put them to sleep. Lift the triangular tail flap on the undersides of the crabs and pull off and discard the top part of the shell. Remove the gills and wash the crabs well. Cut the crabs into quarters if using mud crabs or in half for the swimmer crabs. Crack the large claws with a heavy knife or nutcracker. Transfer the crab to a bowl.

For the green seasoning, place the ingredients and 2 tablespoons water in the small bowl of a food processor and blitz to a paste. Add to the crab and mix well to combine. Set aside to marinate for at least 30 minutes.

To make the dumplings, combine the flour, salt and enough water (about 185 ml/6 fl oz/¾ cup) to form a soft dough. Knead lightly, until soft, then transfer to a bowl, cover with a cloth and set aside.

For the curry, heat the oil in a large heavy-based saucepan over medium heat. Add the onion, garlic and pepper and cook for 5 minutes, or until the onion has softened. Add the spices and stir for 2 minutes, or until the mixture looks 'sandy'. Add the coconut milk, fish stock, chilli and sugar, then stir to combine and simmer for 5 minutes. Add the crab. Cover and cook for 10 minutes, or until the crab changes colour. Season with salt and lime juice, to taste.

On a lightly floured work surface, divide the dough into thirds, then roll each into a sausage shape about 2.5 cm (1 in) wide. Cut each sausage into 10 small pieces and roll into small balls. Add to the curry and simmer until cooked through – they should retain a slight bite. Scatter the curry with coriander leaves and serve.

Singapore curry noodles

Singapore

Place the noodles in a large heatproof bowl and cover with boiling water. Set aside for 5 minutes, or until the noodles have softened, but still have some bite. Drain and set aside to dry out.

To make the sauce, combine all the ingredients in a small bowl and set aside.

Combine the prawns, 1 teaspoon of the peanut oil and the fish sauce in a bowl. Cover and refrigerate until required.

Heat another teaspoon of the oil in a large wok or deep frying pan over high heat until smoking. Add the egg with a pinch of salt. Swirl to cover the base of the wok and cook until the egg starts to set, then gently move the egg back and forth with a spatula until just cooked. Slice the omelette and transfer to a large bowl.

Wipe the wok clean and return to high heat. Add 2 more teaspoons of oil and heat until smoking. Add the shallot, ginger and garlic and stir-fry for 30 seconds, until fragrant. Add the prawns and stir-fry for 1 minute, then add the pork and cook for another 30 seconds. Add the capsicum, carrot, 2 teaspoons of the curry powder and cook, stirring, until the prawns are just cooked through. Transfer the mixture to the bowl with the omelette.

Clean the wok again. Heat the remaining oil over high heat until smoking. Add the softened noodles and stir-fry for 30 seconds. Add the sauce and remaining curry powder. Toss until well combined. Return the prawn and vegetable mixture to the wok and stir-fry for 1 minute, or until well combined and heated through. Remove from the heat, add the bean sprouts and spring onion, drizzle with sesame oil, toss again and serve immediately with lime wedges for squeezing over.

150 g (5½ oz) bundle dried rice vermicelli, broken in half

500 g (1 lb 2 oz) raw green prawns (shrimp), peeled and deveined with tails left intact

3 tablespoons peanut (ground nut) oil

2 teaspoons fish sauce

2 free-range eggs, lightly beaten

2 Asian shallots, thinly sliced

2.5 cm (1 in) piece ginger, julienned

2 garlic cloves, crushed

150 g (5½ oz) Chinese barbecued (char sui) pork, thinly sliced

1 small red capsicum (bell pepper), julienned

1 small carrot, julienned

1 tablespoon all-purpose curry powder

80 g (2¾ oz) bean sprouts, tails trimmed

3 spring onions (scallions), thinly sliced diagonally

2 teaspoons sesame oil

lime wedges, to serve

Sauce

1 teaspoon brown sugar

2 teaspoons fish sauce

1 tablespoon soy sauce

1 tablespoon Shaoxing rice wine

SERVES 2–4

Nasi lemak
Malaysia

60 g (2 oz) ikan bilis (dried anchovies)

80 ml (2½ fl oz) peanut (ground nut) oil

400 g (14 oz/2 cups) jasmine rice

4 pandan leaves, tied in knots

1 lemongrass stalk, pale section only, bruised

3 slices ginger

160 ml (5½ fl oz) coconut milk

½ teaspoon salt, to taste

4 banana leaves, cut into 25 cm (10 in) squares

To serve

Sambal (see page 213)

4 free-range hardboiled eggs, halved

cucumber slices

salted peanuts

lime wedges

SERVES 4

Rinse the dried anchovies and pat dry with paper towel. Heat the oil in a small saucepan over high heat. Add the anchovies and cook, stirring, until golden and crisp. Remove with a slotted spoon and drain on paper towel.

Wash the rice well in a bowl of cold water. Transfer to a colander and rinse with more cold water until the water runs clear. Place the rice in a large saucepan with the pandan leaves, lemongrass, ginger, coconut milk, salt and 580 ml (19½ fl oz) water. Bring to the boil over medium heat, then reduce to a simmer, cover and cook for 15 minutes. Remove from the heat and stand, covered, for 10 minutes. Alternatively, you can cook all the ingredients in a rice cooker. The rice grains should be separate and a little sticky.

To serve, pack the rice tightly into four small rice bowls, then invert onto the banana leaves.

Serve with the fried anchovies, sambal, hard-boiled eggs, cucumber, peanuts and lime wedges for squeezing over.

Tamarind fish curry

Malaysia

80 ml (2½ fl oz/⅓ cup) peanut (ground nut) oil

3 tablespoons tamarind pulp

1 bud ginger flower (torch ginger), finely chopped (see note)

150 g (5½ oz) okra

600 g (1 lb 5 oz) thick firm white fish fillets, cut into 3 cm (1¼ in) pieces

1–2 teaspoons shaved dark coconut sugar, to taste

steamed rice, to serve

Spice paste

5 small dried red chillies (or more if you like it hot)

3 Asian red shallots, roughly chopped

3 candlenuts, macadamias or brazil nuts

1 tablespoon belacan (fermented shrimp paste)

2 cm (¾ in) piece fresh galangal

2 cm (¾ in) piece fresh turmeric, roughly chopped

3 lemongrass stalks, pale section only, peeled and chopped

1 garlic clove

SERVES 4

To make the spice paste, soak the chillies in hot water for 15 minutes, or until softened. Drain. Blend the chillies and remaining spice paste ingredients in the small bowl of a food processor or blender, until finely chopped and a paste is formed.

Heat the oil in a wok or large frying pan over low heat. Add the spice paste and cook, stirring occasionally, for 10–15 minutes, until the oil and paste separate and the mixture is fragrant.

Combine the tamarind pulp and 500 ml (17 fl oz/2 cups) water in a bowl. Mix well to dissolve the tamarind pulp and strain, discarding the seeds and fibres. Add the strained tamarind water to the spice paste and bring to the boil. Simmer over low heat for 10–15 minutes, until thickened slightly. Add the ginger flower, okra and fish. Simmer for 5–7 minutes, until the fish is just cooked through and the okra is tender. Season with a little coconut sugar and salt to balance the taste, if necessary.

Serve with steamed rice.

NOTE: GINGER FLOWER (TORCH GINGER) IS AVAILABLE FROZEN FROM ASIAN GROCERY STORES. IT CAN BE SUBSTITUTED WITH A LITTLE FINELY GRATED GINGER AND VIETNAMESE MINT.

Sri Lankan curried crab

Sri Lanka

2 large mud crabs or 4 blue swimmer
　　crabs, well cleaned

60 ml (2 fl oz/¼ cup) vegetable oil

1 red onion, thinly sliced

4 garlic cloves, finely chopped

4 cm (1½ in) piece ginger, finely chopped

3 small green chillies, finely chopped

2 sprigs curry leaves

1 teaspoon fennel seeds

1 teaspoon black mustard seeds

½ teaspoon fenugreek seeds

1 teaspoon chilli powder

½ teaspoon ground turmeric

400 ml (14 fl oz) tin coconut milk

squeeze of lime juice, to taste

small handful coriander (cilantro) leaves

steamed basmati rice (see page 178),
　　Chapattis (see page 190) or
　　Paratha (see page 191), to serve

Curry powder

2 teaspoons coriander seeds

1 teaspoon cumin seeds

1 teaspoon black peppercorns

1 teaspoon uncooked rice

½ teaspoon black mustard seeds

¾ teaspoon whole cloves

½ teaspoon cardamom seeds

1 teaspoon fennel seeds

SERVES 4

If you've purchased live crabs, place them in the freezer for 1 hour, to put them to sleep.

Lift the triangular tail flap on the undersides of the crabs and pull off and discard the top part of the shell. Remove the gills and wash the crabs well. Cut the crabs into quarters if using mud crabs or in half for the swimmer crabs. Crack the large claws with a heavy knife or nutcracker.

To make the curry powder, grind the spices in a spice grinder or with a mortar and pestle.

Heat the oil in a wok, large heavy-based saucepan or flameproof casserole dish over medium heat. Add the onion, garlic, ginger, chilli, curry leaves and whole spices and cook, stirring occasionally, for 5 minutes. Add the chilli powder, ground turmeric and curry powder and cook for a further 1 minute.

Add the crab and toss to coat in the spices. Pour in the coconut milk and 250 ml (8½ fl oz/1 cup) water, then cover and simmer for 12 minutes, or until the crab is just cooked. Season with salt and a good squeeze of lime juice, to taste.

Scatter the curried crab with coriander leaves and serve with steamed rice, chapattis or paratha on the side.

Goan-style prawn curry
India

1 tablespoon peanut (ground nut) oil
1 onion, finely chopped
1 small tomato, finely chopped
3 garlic cloves, crushed,
2 cm (¾ in) piece ginger, finely grated
2 teaspoons sweet paprika
1 teaspoon ground coriander
½ teaspoon ground cumin
½ teaspoon freshly ground black pepper
½ teaspoon cayenne pepper
300 ml (10½ fl oz) coconut milk
1 kg (2 lb 3 oz) raw green prawns (shrimp),
    peeled and deveined with tails left intact
½ teaspoon salt
1–2 teaspoons tamarind purée, to taste
coriander (cilantro) leaves, to serve
steamed basmati rice (see page 178),
    to serve
lime wedges, to serve

SERVES 4

Heat the oil in a large frying pan over medium heat. Add the onion
and cook, stirring occasionally, for 6–8 minutes, until softened and
starting to brown. Add the tomato and cook for 2 minutes, or until
softened. Add the garlic and ginger and cook until fragrant. Add
the spices and cook, stirring, for a further 2 minutes.

Add the coconut milk and bring to the boil over medium heat.
Reduce the heat to medium–low and bring the sauce to a
simmer. Add the prawns, salt and tamarind purée. Stir and cook
for 4–5 minutes, or until the prawns are just cooked through.

Scatter with coriander and serve with steamed basmati rice and
lime wedges for squeezing over.

Bengali fish curry
India

4 x 150 g–200 g (5½ oz–7 oz) mackerel
  steaks
1 teaspoon ground turmeric
1½ teaspoons black mustard seeds
1½ teaspoons yellow mustard seeds
1 small onion, roughly chopped
8 small green chillies or 4 long green
  chillies
60 ml (2 fl oz/¼ cup) vegetable
  or mustard oil
½ teaspoon salt
4 fresh or dried bay leaves, preferably
  Indian
steamed basmati rice (see page 178),
  to serve

SERVES 4

Rub the fish with a sprinkling of salt and half the turmeric.

Grind the mustard seeds in a spice grinder or with a mortar and pestle. Blend the ground mustard seeds, onion and half the chillies in the small bowl of a food processor or blender to a smooth paste. Add a small amount of water to get the mixture moving, if necessary.

Heat the oil in a medium frying pan over medium–high heat. Cook the fish for 1–2 minutes each side or until lightly browned. Transfer to a plate.

Add the onion paste, remaining turmeric, salt and bay leaves to the pan, then reduce the heat to medium and cook for 3 minutes, or until fragrant. Add 375 ml (12½ fl oz/1½ cups) water and bring to the boil. Simmer for 5 minutes, then return the fish to the pan and add the remaining chillies. Reduce the heat to medium–low and simmer, covered, for 5–6 minutes, or until the fish is just cooked through. Season with a little more salt, if necessary.

Serve with steamed basmati rice.

Chilli crab
Singapore

2 large mud crabs or 4 blue swimmer
  crabs, well cleaned
1 onion, chopped
5 garlic cloves, chopped
3 cm (1¼ in) piece ginger, roughly
  chopped
6–8 long red chillies (depending on how
  hot you like it), chopped
½ teaspoon salt
60 ml (2 fl oz/¼ cup) vegetable oil
1 tablespoon tomato paste (concentrated
  purée)
2 large tomatoes, very finely chopped
  or puréed
125 ml (4 fl oz/½ cup) fish or chicken stock
1½ tablespoons shaved palm sugar
  or brown sugar
1 tablespoon white vinegar
1½ tablespoons soy sauce
1 teaspoon cornflour (corn starch) mixed
  with 2 teaspoons cold water
1 free-range egg, lightly beaten
3 spring onions (scallions), sliced
  diagonally
coriander (cilantro) leaves, to serve
steamed rice, to serve (optional)

SERVES 4

If you've purchased live crabs, place them in the freezer for 1 hour, to put them to sleep.

Lift the triangular tail flap on the undersides of the crabs and pull off and discard the top part of the shell. Remove the gills and wash the crabs well. Cut the crabs into quarters if using mud crabs or in half for the swimmer crabs. Crack the large claws with a heavy knife or nutcracker.

Place the onion, garlic, ginger, chilli and salt in the small bowl of a food processor and blend to a paste.

Heat the oil in a wok over medium–high heat until hot. Add the onion paste and cook for 3–4 minutes, until softened. Add the crab and toss it in the paste. Add the tomato paste, tomato, stock, sugar, vinegar and soy sauce. Stir well and simmer for 2 minutes. Cover the wok and simmer for a further 10 minutes, or until the crab is cooked through. Transfer the crab to a plate.

Add the cornflour mixture and egg to the sauce. Bring just to the boil, stirring, and cook until just thickened. Pour over the crab and sprinkle with the spring onion and coriander. Serve with steamed rice, if you like.

Octopus Curry
Mauritius

1 kg (2 lb 3 oz) octopus, cleaned (ask your fishmonger to do this for you)

1 teaspoon salt

½ teaspoon ground cloves

½ teaspoon ground cinnamon

60 ml (2 fl oz/¼ cup) vegetable oil

1 large onion, finely chopped

4 garlic cloves, finely chopped

3 cm (1¼ in) piece ginger, finely grated

1 long red chilli, sliced

6 curry leaves

1 thyme sprig

2 fresh bay leaves

2 tablespoons mild or Madras curry powder mixed with 60 ml (2 fl oz/¼ cup) water

1 teaspoon ground turmeric

3 whole cloves

1 tablespoon chopped coriander (cilantro) stalks

5 tomatoes, very finely chopped or puréed

coriander (cilantro) leaves, to serve

Roti canai (see page 199) or steamed rice, to serve

SERVES 4

Rub the octopus all over with the salt, ground cloves and cinnamon.

Place the octopus in a large saucepan over low heat and allow to simmer in its own juices for 10–15 minutes, or until pink. Remove from the pan and set aside to cool. Cut the octopus into small bite-sized pieces.

Heat the oil in a large frying pan or heavy-based saucepan over medium heat. Add the onion, garlic, ginger, chilli, curry leaves, thyme and bay leaves, reduce the heat to low and cook for 5 minutes. Add the curry powder mixture, turmeric, cloves and coriander stems and stir for 1–2 minutes.

Add the tomato and simmer, covered, for 20 minutes until thick and the oil has started to separate. Add a little water if the mixture becomes very thick. Add the octopus and cook for a further 15–20 minutes, until tender.

Scatter the curry with coriander leaves and serve with roti or steamed rice.

1 kg (2 lb 3 oz) raw green prawns (shrimp)

400 ml (13½ fl oz) tin coconut milk (do not shake before opening)

1 tablespoon peanut (ground nut) oil

3 tablespoons Green curry paste (see page 207)

1 teaspoon grated palm sugar, plus extra to taste

250 ml (8½ fl oz/1 cup) chicken stock

2 tablespoons fish sauce, plus extra to taste

100 g (3½ oz) baby corn, halved lengthways

½ small (about 200 g/7 oz) daikon (white radish), julienned

2 long red chillies, thinly sliced diagonally

4 kaffir lime leaves, torn

handful Thai basil leaves

steamed jasmine rice (see page 178), to serve

SERVES 4

Prawn green curry
Thailand

Peel and devein the prawns, leaving the tails intact and reserving the heads. Rinse the heads well and discard only the hard shell at the top.

Scoop 3 tablespoons of the thick cream from the top of the coconut milk tin and place in a medium saucepan. Add the oil and cook over medium heat until bubbling. Add the curry paste and cook, stirring constantly, for 3–4 minutes, or until very aromatic. Add the sugar, remaining coconut milk, stock and fish sauce. Bring to the boil, reduce the heat to a simmer and cook for about 3 minutes, or until fragrant.

Add the baby corn and simmer for 2 minutes. Add the prawns, prawn heads and daikon and cook for 4–5 minutes, until the prawns are just cooked through. Season to taste with more fish sauce and sugar to balance the flavour, if necessary.

Scatter over the chilli, limes leaves and Thai basil, and serve with steamed jasmine rice.

1 kg–1.5 kg (2 lb 3 oz–3 lb 5 oz) fish heads, such as ling or snapper

2 teaspoons salt

60 ml (2 fl oz/¼ cup) vegetable oil

3 sprigs curry leaves, plus extra to fry

500 ml (17 fl oz/2 cups) coconut milk

2 tablespoons tamarind purée, plus extra to taste

1 teaspoon sugar, plus extra to taste

10 small okra

2 tomatoes, cut into wedges

steamed jasmine rice (see page 178), to serve

Fish curry powder

4 teaspoons ground coriander

1 tablespoon ground cumin

1 teaspoon ground fennel

1 teaspoon chilli powder

1 teaspoon ground turmeric

½ teaspoon freshly ground black pepper

Spice paste

1 tablespoon belacan (fermented shrimp paste)

2 red onions, roughly chopped

2 long red chillies, seeded and coarsely chopped

4 cm (1½ in) piece ginger, coarsely chopped

2 cm (¾ in) piece fresh galangal, finely grated

1 lemongrass stalk, pale section only, thinly sliced

3 garlic cloves

1 tablespoon vegetable oil

SERVES 4

Fish head curry
Malaysia

Combine all the ingredients for the fish curry powder in a small bowl and set aside.

Rinse the fish heads in cold water to remove any traces of blood, then sprinkle with the salt and set aside for 20 minutes. Wash off the salt and pat dry with paper towel, then rub 1 tablespoon of the curry powder into the fish heads. Set aside.

To make the spice paste, wrap the belacan in foil and cook in a dry frying pan, turning the package every now and then, for 3 minutes, or until fragrant. Transfer to a blender, along with the remaining spice paste ingredients and blend to a paste. Add a little water to get the mixture moving if necessary.

Heat the oil in a wok or large frying pan over medium–high heat. Add the extra curry leaves (about 3 sprigs) and fry for a few seconds until crisp. Remove from the pan, drain on paper towel and reserve for a garnish. Add the fish heads to the pan and cook for 2–3 minutes on each side, until lightly browned. Transfer to a plate and set aside. Add the spice paste and remaining curry powder to the pan and cook for 3 minutes, or until fragrant and the oil separates from the paste. Stir in the curry leaves, then add the coconut milk, tamarind purée and sugar. Bring to the boil, then reduce the heat to low and simmer for 5 minutes.

Place the fish heads in the sauce, adding boiling water if necessary to the bring the liquid halfway up the height of the fish. Reduce the heat to low and simmer, turning the fish over halfway through the cooking time, for 8–10 minutes. Add the okra and tomato and simmer for a further 3–5 minutes, until the okra is just tender and the fish is cooked through. Season to taste with extra tamarind, sugar and salt. Scatter with the reserved curry leaves and serve with steamed jasmine rice.

Mussels in coconut curry broth
Thailand

400 ml (13½ fl oz) tin coconut milk (do not shake before opening)
1 tablespoon peanut (ground nut) oil
3 garlic cloves, thinly sliced
1 Asian shallot, thinly sliced
3 tablespoons Red curry paste (see page 206)
1 tablespoon grated palm sugar
4 kaffir lime leaves, torn
1 tablespoon fish sauce, plus extra to taste
1 kg (2 lb 3 oz) mussels, scrubbed and debearded
1 tablespoon freshly squeezed lime juice
handful fresh coriander (cilantro), roughly chopped
1 small Thai green chilli, thinly sliced
steamed jasmine rice (see page 178), to serve
lime wedges, to serve

SERVES 4

Scoop 2 tablespoons of the thick cream from the top of the coconut milk tin and place in a large wide saucepan. Add the oil and heat over medium heat until sputtering. Add the garlic, shallot and curry paste. Cook, stirring constantly, for 3–4 minutes, until very aromatic. Add the remaining coconut milk, sugar, lime leaves and fish sauce. Bring to a simmer and cook for about 3 minutes, or until fragrant. Season to taste with more fish sauce to balance the flavour if necessary.

Add the mussels, stir, cover and cook, shaking the pan constantly and giving it a stir every 30 seconds or so. Quickly scoop out any mussels that are open and place them in a large bowl. As soon as all the mussels are open (discard any that don't), return all the open mussels to the pan, stir in the lime juice and scatter with the coriander and chilli. Serve immediately with steamed rice and lime wedges for squeezing over.

400 ml (13½ fl oz) tin coconut milk
    or cream

1 tablespoon fish sauce

2 tablespoons shaved palm sugar

1 free-range egg, lightly beaten

4 x 150 g (5½ oz) skinless firm white
    fish fillets

12 large raw prawns (shrimp), peeled and
    deveined, tails left intact

4 banana leaves, cut into 25 cm (10 in)
    squares

finely shredded kaffir lime leaves, to serve

thinly sliced long red chillies, to serve

steamed rice, to serve

Curry paste

1 teaspoon belacan (fermented
    shrimp paste)

3 long dried red chillies, soaked in warm
    water for 15 minutes, drained

2 lemongrass stalks, pale section only,
    peeled and chopped

4 garlic cloves, peeled

2 Asian shallots, chopped

1 tablespoon chopped galangal

2 teaspoons freshly grated turmeric

zest of 2 kaffir limes (use the zest of
    1 lime and 2 double kaffir lime leaves
    if unavailable)

SERVES 4

Seafood amok
Cambodia

To make the curry paste, wrap the belacan in foil and cook in a dry frying pan or under a hot grill (broiler), turning the package every now and then, for 3 minutes, or until fragrant. Transfer the belacan to a mortar and pestle or the small bowl of a food processor, along with the rest of the curry paste ingredients and pound or process to a paste.

Heat a dry frying pan over low heat and fry the paste for 2 minutes. Add the coconut milk, reserving 2 tablespoons for garnish. Add the fish sauce and sugar and simmer for 1 minute. Transfer the mixture to a bowl and set aside to cool. Stir in the egg and add the fish and prawns.

Lay the banana leaves on a flat surface and evenly spoon the fish and prawn mixture on the leaves. Fold in the edges to make a parcel and enclose the filling. Secure with string or toothpicks, if necessary.

Set a large steamer over a saucepan of boiling water and add the fish parcels. Steam for 15–20 minutes, or until just cooked through. Remove the parcels from the steamer.

Open the banana leaves and drizzle over the reserved coconut milk. Scatter the shredded kaffir lime leaves and chilli on top of the amok and serve with steamed rice.

Prawn malai curry
India

60 ml (2 fl oz/¼ cup) mustard oil or ghee

1 large cinnamon stick

2 fresh or dried bay leaves (preferably Indian)

2 medium onions, finely chopped

4 cm (1¼ in) piece ginger, finely grated

4 garlic cloves, crushed

1 teaspoon cumin seeds

1 teaspoon chilli powder (preferably Kashmiri)

2 teaspoons ground turmeric

24 large raw prawns (shrimp), peeled and deveined, tails left intact

500 ml (17 fl oz/2 cups) coconut milk

1 teaspoon salt

½ teaspoon sugar

1 teaspoon Garam masala (see page 218 or use store-bought)

lime or lemon wedges, to serve

steamed basmati rice (see page 178), to serve

SERVES 4

Heat the oil in heavy-based saucepan or large frying pan over medium heat. Add the cinnamon stick and bay leaves and cook for 1 minute. Reduce the heat to low, add the onion and cook for 10 minutes, until soft and slightly coloured. Add the ginger and garlic and cook for a further 2 minutes. Add the spices, followed by the prawns and stir for 1 minute.

Add the coconut milk, 80 ml (2½ fl oz/⅓ cup) water, the salt and sugar and simmer for 5 minutes, or until the prawns are cooked through. Sprinkle over the garam masala.

Serve with lime or lemon wedges for squeezing over and steamed basmati rice on the side.

Sour orange fish curry
Thailand

1 teaspoon Thai shrimp paste

7 long dried red chillies, soaked in hot water for 15–20 minutes, drained

1 teaspoon salt

3 large Asian shallots, peeled

750 ml (25½ fl oz/3 cups) fish or chicken stock

1 lemongrass stalk, pale section only, bruised

6 kaffir lime leaves

4 x 100 g (3½ oz) skinless firm white fish fillets

100 g (3½ oz) baby corn

100 g (3½ oz) choy sum, leaves separated

100 g (3½ oz) snake (yard-long) beans, cut into 3 cm (1¼ in lengths)

2 tomatoes, cut into wedges

3 tablespoons tamarind purée, to taste

2 tablespoons fish sauce, to taste

1½–2 teaspoons sugar, to taste

steamed jasmine rice (see page 178), to serve

SERVES 4

Wrap the shrimp paste in foil and cook in a dry frying pan or under a hot grill (broiler), turning the package every now and then, for 3 minutes, or until fragrant. Transfer the shrimp paste to a mortar and pestle or the small bowl of a food processor, along with the chillies, salt and one shallot and pound or process to a paste.

Combine the paste, remaining whole shallots, stock, lemongrass and kaffir lime leaves in a large saucepan or frying pan. Bring to the boil. Add the fish, baby corn, choy sum, snake beans and tomato and simmer gently until just cooked.

Season the curry with the tamarind purée, fish sauce and sugar to create a sour, hot and very slightly sweet flavour. Serve with steamed jasmine rice on the side.

Poultry

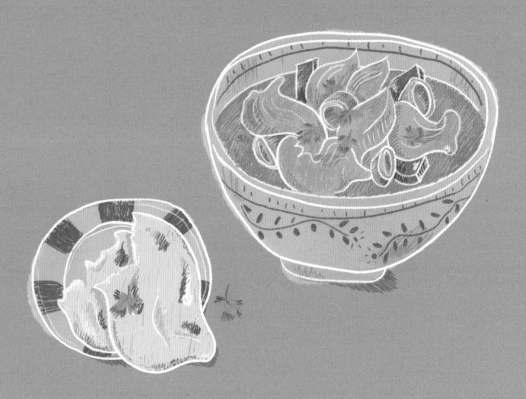

Butter chicken

India

Using a heavy cleaver or sharp knife, cut the chicken cutlets in half. Combine the chicken, yoghurt and tandoori curry paste in a large bowl. Cover and refrigerate for 30 minutes to 2 hours.

Heat a chargrill pan, barbecue grill or heavy-based frying pan over high heat. Shake the excess marinade from the chicken and cook for 3–4 minutes on each side, until well charred in spots, but not cooked through. Transfer to a plate and set aside.

Meanwhile, heat the ghee and oil in a large heavy-based frying pan over medium–low heat. Add the onion and salt and cook, stirring occasionally, for 10–15 minutes, until the onion is a rich golden brown. Add the ginger and garlic and cook, stirring, for 2 minutes, or until fragrant. Add the chilli powder, turmeric and green chilli and cook for a further 1 minute. Add the passata, then bring to the boil over medium heat and simmer, uncovered and stirring often, for 5–10 minutes, until the tomato is reduced and slightly thickened.

Place the cashew nuts in the small bowl of a food processor and process until finely ground.

Add the cream and butter to the tomato mixture and cook, stirring, until the butter is melted. Stir in the ground cashews, charred chicken, honey and fenugreek leaves, and cook, stirring frequently, for 5–6 minutes, until the chicken is cooked through. Add a little boiling water to thin the consistency, if the sauce is very thick. Stir in the coriander and season, to taste.

Serve the butter chicken with naan on the side.

8 (about 1.5 kg/3 lb 5 oz) skin-on chicken thigh cutlets
125 g (4½ oz/½ cup) plain yoghurt
3 tablespoons Tandoori curry paste (see page 216)
2 tablespoons ghee
2 tablespoons vegetable oil
2 large onions, chopped
1 teaspoon salt
3 cm (1¼ in) piece ginger, finely grated
2 garlic cloves, crushed
1 teaspoon chilli powder
2 teaspoons ground turmeric
1 long green chilli, chopped
425 g (15 oz) passata (puréed tomatoes)
75 g (2¾ oz/½ cup) raw cashew nuts
180 ml (6 fl oz) cream
40 g (1½ oz) unsalted butter, chopped
4 teaspoons honey
1 tablespoon dried fenugreek leaves
small handful coriander (cilantro), roughly chopped
Simple naan (see page 194), to serve

SERVES 4

Chicken tandoori

India

1.5 kg (3 lb 5 oz) whole chicken
180 g (6½ oz/¾ cup) plain yoghurt
125 g (4½ oz/½ cup) Tandoori curry paste
(see page 216)
coriander (cilantro) leaves, to serve
lemon wedges, to serve
Simple naan (see page 194), to serve

SERVES 4

First, butterfly or flatten the chicken. Using kitchen scissors, cut along both sides of the backbone and remove. Turn the chicken over and place on a clean, flat work surface. Using the heels of your hands, press down firmly on the breastbone to flatten.

Slash the chicken about 1 cm (½ in) deep through the thickest part of the breast, thighs and legs.

Combine the yoghurt and tandoori curry paste in a bowl, then rub all over the chicken, rubbing well into the slashed areas. Transfer to a baking tray lined with baking paper, then cover and marinate in the fridge for 2–4 hours.

Preheat the oven to 240°C (450°F) fan-forced.

Roast the chicken for 30 minutes, or until it starts to char in spots. Reduce the oven temperature to 150°C (300°F) fan-forced and roast for a further 5–10 minutes, until cooked through. Remove from the oven and set aside to rest, covered loosely with foil, for 10 minutes.

Scatter the coriander over the chicken and serve with lemon wedges for squeezing over and naan on the side.

70 g (2½ oz/½ cup) raw peanuts
(ground nuts) (see note)

3 tablespoons Panang curry paste
(see page 211)

400 ml (13½ fl oz) tin coconut milk (do
not shake before opening)

1 tablespoon peanut (ground nut) oil

2 tablespoons grated palm sugar, plus
extra to taste

125 ml (4 fl oz/½ cup) chicken stock

2 tablespoons fish sauce, plus extra to taste

600 g (1 lb 5 oz) skinless chicken thigh
fillets, cut into 2 cm (¾ in) pieces

1 long red chilli, thinly sliced

4 kaffir lime leaves, finely shredded

Thai basil leaves, to serve

steamed jasmine rice (see page 178),
to serve

SERVES 4

Panang chicken curry
Thailand

Toast the peanuts in a large dry frying pan over medium heat, stirring often, for 3–4 minutes, until the skins loosen and the nuts become fragrant and lightly browned in spots. Set aside to cool slightly, then use a clean tea towel to rub off the skins and discard. Allow the peanuts to cool completely, then pound or blend to a paste and combine them with the curry paste in a small bowl.

Scoop 3 tablespoons of the thick cream from the top of the coconut milk tin and place in a medium saucepan. Add the oil and cook over medium heat until bubbling. Add the curry paste mixture and cook, stirring constantly, for 4–5 minutes, until very aromatic. Add the sugar and stir for 1 minute, then add the remaining coconut milk, stock and fish sauce.

Add the chicken and bring to the boil, then reduce the heat to low and simmer for 10–15 minutes, until the chicken is tender and the sauce has thickened. If the sauce is still very thin, use a slotted spoon to transfer the chicken to a bowl and continue to simmer the sauce for 5–10 minutes, until reduced and thickened to your liking. Return the chicken to the sauce and heat through for 1–2 minutes. The end result should be a fairly dry curry.

Season to taste with extra fish sauce and palm sugar to balance the flavours, if necessary. Scatter the chilli, kaffir lime leaves and basil over the top and serve with steamed jasmine rice.

NOTE: IF YOU CAN'T FIND RAW PEANUTS (GROUND NUTS), USE UNSALTED ROASTED PEANUTS INSTEAD.

Kuku paka

Kenya

4 (about 1.5 kg/3 lb 5 oz) chicken legs (marylands)
4 garlic cloves, crushed
3 cm (1¼ in) piece ginger, finely grated
2 long green chillies, chopped (seeded if you prefer less heat)
2 teaspoons ground turmeric
2 teaspoons ground coriander
1 teaspoon ground cumin
½ teaspoon chilli powder
½ teaspoon salt
400 ml (13½ fl oz) tin coconut milk
2 tablespoons tamarind purée
coriander (cilantro) leaves, roughly chopped, to serve (optional)
lemon wedges, to serve
steamed rice or flatbreads, to serve

Marinade
juice of 1 lemon
2 garlic cloves, crushed
2 cm (¾ in) piece ginger, finely grated
1 teaspoon vegetable oil

SERVES 4

Using a sharp knife, cut the chicken legs between the thighs and drumsticks. You will have eight pieces of chicken.

To make the marinade, combine the ingredients in a large bowl. Add the chicken pieces and mix well, then cover and marinate in the fridge for 1–2 hours.

Heat a chargrill pan, barbecue grill or heavy-based frying pan over high heat. Shake the excess marinade from the chicken and cook, turning occasionally, for 8–10 minutes, until well charred in spots, but not quite cooked through. Transfer to a plate and set aside.

Combine the garlic, ginger, fresh chilli, spices, salt and coconut milk in a large saucepan over medium–low heat. Bring to the boil, then reduce the heat to low and simmer, stirring frequently, for 10–15 minutes, until slightly thickened. Stir in the tamarind purée and charred chicken, adding a little water, if necessary, to half cover the chicken. Bring to the boil again, then reduce the heat and simmer, covered and stirring occasionally, for 10–15 minutes, until the chicken is cooked through and the sauce is slightly thickened. Scatter over the coriander, if using.

Serve with lemon wedges for squeezing over and steamed rice or flatbreads.

Chicken balti

India

2 tablespoons ghee or vegetable oil

2 teaspoons black mustard seeds

1 red capsicum (bell pepper), cut into 1.5 cm (½ in) pieces

1 large onion, chopped

4 long green chillies, halved lengthways

1 fresh or dried bay leaf (preferably Indian)

5 garlic cloves, crushed

3 cm (1¼ in) piece ginger, finely grated

400 g (14 oz) tin crushed tomatoes

60 g (2 oz/¼ cup) plain yoghurt

1 tablespoon besan (chickpea flour)

2 teaspoons Garam masala (see page 218 or use store-bought)

2 teaspoons ground coriander

2 teaspoons ground cumin

1 teaspoon Kashmiri chilli powder

1 teaspoon ground turmeric

½ teaspoon salt

600 g (1 lb 5 oz) skinless chicken thigh fillets, cut into 2.5 cm (1 in) pieces

squeeze of lemon juice, to taste

coriander (cilantro) leaves, roughly chopped, to serve

steamed basmati rice (see page 178), to serve

SERVES 4

Heat the ghee or oil in a large heavy-based saucepan over medium heat. Add the mustard seeds and sizzle for a few seconds. When they start to crackle, add the capsicum, onion, green chilli and bay leaf. Cook, stirring occasionally, for 10–12 minutes, until golden and starting to stick to the base of the pan. Add the garlic and ginger and cook, stirring, for about 30 seconds, or until fragrant.

Add the tomato, yoghurt, besan, spices and salt and stir until well combined. Bring to the boil, then reduce the heat to medium–low and simmer for 10 minutes, or until slightly thickened.

Add the chicken and stir well to coat in the sauce. Return the mixture to the boil over medium heat, then reduce the heat to a simmer and cook, covered and stirring occasionally, for 15–20 minutes, until the chicken is cooked through and the sauce has thickened.

Season, to taste with lemon juice, freshly ground black pepper and a little more salt, if necessary.

Scatter the curry with the coriander and serve with steamed basmati rice on the side.

Singapore chicken curry

Singapore

1 kg (2 lb 3 oz) skinless chicken thigh cutlets

6 Asian shallots, chopped

5 cm (2 in) piece ginger, finely grated

5 garlic cloves, crushed

80 ml (2½ fl oz/⅓ cup) vegetable or peanut (ground nut) oil

500 ml (17 fl oz/2 cups) coconut milk (or use half coconut milk and half coconut cream)

500 g (1 lb 2 oz) small potatoes, peeled and halved, or large potatoes cut into large chunks

1 teaspoon salt

1 teaspoon sugar

juice of 1 lime

steamed jasmine rice (see page 178) or Roti canai (see page 199), to serve

Curry powder

2 dried red chillies, halved (seeded if you prefer less heat)

3 teaspoons coriander seeds

1½ teaspoons cumin seeds

1 small cinnamon stick

4 cardamom pods, seeds only

12 whole cloves

½ teaspoon black peppercorns

1½ teaspoons fennel seeds

1 teaspoon ground turmeric

SERVES 4

To make the curry powder, combine all the ingredients except the turmeric in a dry frying pan over low heat and cook for 2 minutes, or until fragrant. Transfer to a spice grinder with the turmeric and blend to a fine powder. Transfer the powder to a large bowl and combine with 60 ml (2 fl oz/¼ cup) water. Add the chicken and toss to coat well in the spice mixture.

Combine the shallot, ginger and garlic in the small bowl of a food processor and blend to a paste.

Heat the oil in a large frying pan or heavy-based saucepan over high heat. Add the chicken and brown on all sides.

Reduce the heat to medium and add the shallot mixture to the pan, along with the coconut milk, potato, salt and sugar. Reduce the heat to low and gently simmer for 20 minutes, or until the chicken is cooked through. Squeeze in the lime juice.

Serve with steamed jasmine rice or roti.

Chinese takeaway curry

U.K.

Combine the bicarbonate of soda with 1 tablespoon water in a medium bowl. Add the chicken and toss to coat. Set aside at room temperature for 5 minutes.

Whisk the soy sauce, 1 tablespoon of the Shaoxing rice wine, 2 teaspoons of the cornflour and 1 teaspoon of the sugar in a small bowl. Add to the chicken mixture, stir to coat, and marinate at room temperature for 15–20 minutes.

Whisk the remaining Shaoxing rice wine, cornflour, sugar, the curry powder, five-spice and stock together in a bowl. Set aside.

Heat a small splash of the oil in a large wok or deep frying pan over high heat until very hot and just smoking. Add half the chicken and stir-fry for 3 minutes, or until lightly browned all over and just cooked through. Transfer to a plate. Repeat with a little more oil and the remaining chicken.

Bring a small saucepan of water to the boil. Place the broccoli in a steamer and steam for 2 minutes.

Return the wok or frying pan to high heat, add a little more oil and heat until the oil begins to smoke. Add the onion, capsicum and steamed broccoli and cook, stirring occasionally, for about 4 minutes, until the vegetables are browned in spots and tender-crisp. Return the chicken and any juices to the wok or pan and add the garlic and ginger. Stir-fry for about 1 minute, or until fragrant.

Whisk the reserved sauce again to combine, then add to the wok or pan and cook, stirring constantly, for 1 minute, or until the sauce thickens.

Serve with prawn crackers and steamed rice on the side.

¼ teaspoon bicarbonate of soda (baking soda)

500 g (1 lb 2 oz) skinless chicken breast or thigh fillets, thinly sliced

1 tablespoon soy sauce

60 ml (2 fl oz/¼ cup) Shaoxing rice wine

5 teaspoons cornflour (corn starch)

1 tablespoon brown sugar

1 tablespoon all-purpose curry

1 teaspoon Chinese five-spice powder

180 ml (6 fl oz) chicken stock

2–3 tablespoons peanut (ground nut) or vegetable oil

1 head broccoli, cut into florets, stem thinly sliced

1 onion, cut into thick wedges

1 red capsicum (bell pepper), cut into 2.5 cm (1 in) diamonds

2 garlic cloves, crushed

2 cm (¾ in) piece ginger, grated

prawn crackers, to serve

steamed rice, to serve

SERVES 4

Chicken katsu curry
Japan

2 x 250 g (9 oz) skinless chicken
  breast fillets
50 g (1¾ oz/⅓ cup) plain (all-purpose)
  flour, seasoned
2 free-range eggs, lightly beaten
90 g (3 oz/1½ cups) panko breadcrumbs
peanut (ground nut) oil, for shallow-frying
steamed rice, to serve
1 x quantity Katsu curry sauce (see
  page 215), warmed
1 spring onion (scallion), thinly sliced
  diagonally, to serve

SERVES 4

Slice each chicken breast fillet in half horizontally. You should have two slices of chicken from each fillet roughly the same size. Place the chicken slices between two sheets of non-stick baking paper. Gently pound the fillets to about 1 cm (½ in) thick.

Place the flour, egg and breadcrumbs in separate bowls. Dip the chicken in the flour, then the egg and finally the breadcrumbs, shaking off any excess mixture between each coating. Heat enough oil to just cover the base of a large frying pan over medium–high heat. Add the chicken and fry, turning occasionally, for 3–4 minutes, until golden and cooked through. Transfer to a plate and cut into thick slices.

Divide the steamed rice and chicken among plates, top with the katsu curry sauce and scatter the spring onion over the top. Serve immediately.

Doro wat
Ethiopia

Joint the chicken, discarding any excess fat. Using a heavy cleaver, cut each piece of chicken through the bone into 4–5 cm (1½–2 in) pieces. You should have about 20 pieces of chicken. Season the chicken with a little salt and freshly ground black pepper and combine with the lemon juice in a medium bowl. Cover and set aside.

To make the nit'r kibbeh, heat the butter, garlic, cinnamon, cardamom and cloves in a small saucepan over very low heat. Simmer very gently for about 30 minutes, skimming any foam from the surface and being careful not to burn the milk solids in the base of the pan. Carefully strain the butter through a fine sieve or piece of muslin (cheesecloth) over a bowl, leaving the milk solids in the bottom of the pan. Stir the fenugreek and nigella into the clarified butter in the bowl. (Any left-over nit'r kibbeh will keep in a sterilised jar in the fridge for up to 1 month.)

Heat the nit'r kibbeh or butter and oil in a large heavy-based saucepan over medium–low heat. Add the onion and cook, covered and stirring occasionally, for 45 minutes, or until very soft and starting to stick to the bottom of the pan. Stir in the berbere, garlic, ginger, tomato paste and paprika and cook, stirring often, for 4–5 minutes, until fragrant.

Add the marinated chicken pieces and any juices from the bowl to the pan, along with the chicken stock. Stir to combine and add a little more water, if necessary, to ensure that the chicken is just covered. Bring to the boil over medium–high heat, then reduce the heat and simmer, covered and stirring occasionally, for 25 minutes, or until the chicken is tender and the sauce has thickened.

Pierce the eggs all over with a fork and gently stir them into the doro wat. Cook, uncovered, for a further 5 minutes, or until the eggs are heated through. Season, to taste.

Serve with injera and steamed rice.

1.5 kg (3 lb 5 oz) whole chicken

juice of 1 lemon

50 g (1¾ oz) nit'r kibbeh (see below) or unsalted butter

60 ml (2 fl oz/¼ cup) vegetable oil

4 onions, finely chopped

40 g (1½ oz/¼ cup) Berbere spice mix (see page 219)

4 garlic cloves, crushed

2 cm (¾ oz) piece ginger, finely grated

1 tablespoon tomato paste (concentrated purée)

2 teaspoons sweet paprika

250 ml (8½ fl oz/1 cup) chicken stock

4 free-range eggs, hardboiled and peeled

Injera (see page 193) and steamed rice, to serve

Nit'r kibbeh

125 g (4 oz) unsalted butter

1 garlic clove, crushed

2 cm (¾ in) piece cinnamon stick

2 cardamom pods, bruised

2 whole cloves

¼ teaspoon ground fenugreek

¼ teaspoon nigella seeds, ground

SERVES 6

Duck red curry
Thailand

4 duck legs (marylands)

2 x 400 ml (13½ fl oz) tins coconut milk
(do not shake before opening)

2 tablespoons peanut (ground nut) oil

75 g (2¾ oz/¼ cup) Red curry paste
(see page 206)

2 long red chillies, thinly sliced diagonally

1 tablespoon fish sauce, plus extra to taste

1 tablespoon lime juice, plus extra to taste

2 teaspoons grated palm sugar, plus extra
to taste

4 apple eggplants (aubergines), each cut
into 6 wedges

100 g (3½ oz) pea eggplants (aubergines)

4 kaffir lime leaves, torn

Thai basil leaves, to serve

steamed jasmine rice (see page 178),
to serve

SERVES 4

Cut the duck legs between the thighs and drumsticks. Using a heavy cleaver, cut each section in half again through the bone. You will have 16 pieces of duck in total.

Scoop 3 tablespoons of the thick cream from the top of the coconut milk tins and place in a large saucepan. Add the oil and heat over medium heat until sputtering. Add the curry paste and cook, stirring constantly, for 3–4 minutes, until very aromatic. Add the duck pieces and cook, stirring, until the duck skin is browned. Add the chilli, fish sauce, lime juice, sugar and remaining coconut milk. Bring to the boil over medium heat, then reduce the heat to medium–low and simmer for 20 minutes, or until the duck is just cooked through. Add the eggplants and lime leaves and cook for a further 5–10 minutes, until tender.

Season to taste with extra fish sauce, lime juice and palm sugar to balance the flavour, if necessary.

Scatter the basil leaves over the top and serve with steamed jasmine rice on the side.

Chicken tikka masala
India

1 kg (2 lb 3 oz) skinless chicken thigh
 fillets, cut into 4 cm (1½ in) pieces

125 g (4½ oz/½ cup) plain yoghurt, plus
 extra to serve

3 tablespoons Tandoori curry paste (see
 page 216)

2 tablespoons ghee

2 tablespoons vegetable oil

2 onions, chopped

4 garlic cloves, crushed

3 cm (1¼ in) piece ginger, finely grated

2 long green chillies, sliced

½ teaspoon salt

1 tablespoon ground coriander

2 teaspoons ground turmeric

2 teaspoons sweet paprika

1 teaspoon Garam masala (see
 page 218 or use store-bought)

400 g (14 oz) tin crushed tomatoes

400 ml (13½ fl oz) tin coconut milk

60 g (2 oz/½ cup) ground almonds

small handful coriander (cilantro), roughly
 chopped, plus extra to serve

2 tablespoons flaked almonds, toasted

Chapattis (see page 190) and/or steamed
 basmati rice (see page 178), to serve

SERVES 4

Combine the chicken, yoghurt and tandoori curry paste in a large bowl. Cover and refrigerate for 30 minutes to 2 hours.

Heat a chargrill pan, barbecue grill or heavy-based frying pan over high heat. Shake the excess marinade from the chicken and cook for 3–4 minutes on each side, until well charred in spots, but not cooked through. Transfer to a plate and set aside.

Heat the ghee and oil in a large heavy-based frying pan over medium–low heat. Add the onion, garlic, ginger, green chilli and salt and cook, stirring occasionally, for 10–15 minutes, until the onion is a rich golden brown. Add the spices and cook, stirring, for a further 1 minute, or until fragrant.

Add the tomato, then bring to the boil over medium heat and simmer, uncovered and stirring often, for 5–10 minutes, until slightly thickened. Stir in the coconut milk and simmer for a further 15–20 minutes, until thickened a little further and the spices have mellowed.

Stir in the ground almonds and charred chicken and cook, stirring often, for 5–6 minutes, until the chicken is cooked through. Add a little boiling water to thin the consistency, if the sauce is very thick.

Stir in the coriander and season, to taste.

Scatter over the flaked almonds and extra coriander, and serve with yoghurt, chapattis and/or steamed basmati rice on the side.

80 ml (½ fl oz/⅓ cup) peanut (ground nut) oil

1.6–1.7 kg (3½ lb–3 lb 12 oz) whole chicken

2 onions, finely chopped

4 garlic cloves, finely chopped

3 long green chillies, chopped

½ teaspoon cumin seeds

1 teaspoon coriander seeds

8 cardamom pods, seeds only

½ teaspoon ground turmeric

3 medium green or red tomatoes, chopped

400 ml (13½ fl oz) tin coconut cream

400 ml (13½ fl oz) tin coconut milk

175 g (6 oz) green beans, trimmed and halved

juice of 1 lime

basil leaves, to serve

steamed rice, to serve

SERVES 4

NOTE: FOR A LIGHTER CURRY, SUBSTITUTE COCONUT MILK FOR THE COCONUT CREAM OR USE HALF CHICKEN STOCK, HALF COCONUT CREAM.

Zanzibar chicken
Tanzania

Joint the chicken, discarding any excess fat. Using a heavy cleaver, cut each piece of chicken through the bone into 4–5 cm (1½–2 in) pieces. You should have about 20 pieces of chicken.

Heat 2 tablespoons of the oil in a large heavy-based saucepan or frying pan with a lid over high heat. Add the chicken and cook, turning frequently, until brown on all sides. Transfer to a plate.

Add the remaining oil to the pan, then reduce the heat to medium and add the onion, garlic and chilli and cook over low heat for 10 minutes, or until the onion is soft.

Meanwhile, very lightly toast the cumin and coriander seeds in a dry frying pan over medium heat, then grind with the cardamom seeds using a mortar and pestle or spice grinder. Add the spice mix to the pan, along with the turmeric and give everything a stir.

Return the chicken to the pan and add the tomato, coconut cream and coconut milk. Gently simmer, partially covered, for 30 minutes, or until the chicken is cooked through. Add the beans and simmer for a further 5 minutes, or until just cooked. Squeeze over the lime juice and season, to taste, with salt.

Scatter over the basil leaves and serve with steamed rice.

Jamaican curried chicken

Jamaica

3 tablespoons Jamaican or all-purpose curry powder

½ teaspoon ground allspice

1 tablespoon vegetable oil

8 (about 1.5 g/3 lb 5 oz) skin-on chicken thigh cutlets

2 onions, sliced

1 red capsicum (bell pepper), cut into 2 cm (¾ in) pieces

3 tablespoons tomato paste (concentrated purée)

4 garlic cloves, crushed

3 cm (1¼ in) piece ginger, finely grated

½ teaspoon freshly ground black pepper

2 fresh thyme sprigs

1–2 Scotch bonnet or other hot chillies, pricked all over with the tip of a knife

500 ml (17 fl oz/2 cups) chicken stock

2 potatoes, cut into 1.5 cm (½ in) thick slices

200 g (7 oz) green beans, trimmed and cut into 4 cm (1½ in) lengths

flatbreads or steamed rice, to serve

SERVES 4

Toast the curry powder and allspice in a small dry frying pan over medium heat, shaking the pan constantly, for 1–2 minutes, until fragrant and slightly darkened in colour. Set aside.

Heat the oil in a large heavy-based saucepan over medium–high heat. Working in batches, cook the chicken for 4–5 minutes, until well browned all over. Transfer to a plate.

Add the onion to the saucepan, then reduce the heat to medium and cook for 5–6 minutes, until lightly browned and soft. Add the capsicum, tomato paste, garlic, ginger, black pepper and roasted curry powder mixture and cook, stirring continuously, for 1 minute. Return the chicken to the pan, add the thyme and chilli and pour over the stock. Stir to combine and add a little water if necessary, to just cover the chicken.

Bring to the boil over medium heat, then reduce the heat to a simmer and cook, covered, for 15 minutes. Add the potato and simmer, uncovered for 15–20 minutes, until the chicken and potato are tender and the sauce is reduced and slightly thickened. Allow the potato to break down slightly to further thicken the sauce, if you like. Add the beans in the last 5 minutes or so of cooking.

Serve with flatbreads or steamed rice on the side.

Ca ri ga
Vietnam

4 (about 1.5 kg/3 lb 5 oz) chicken legs (marylands)
1 teaspoon garlic powder
1 teaspoon onion powder
½ teaspoon salt
2 tablespoons all-purpose curry powder
60 ml (2 fl oz/¼ cup) vegetable oil
1 onion, cut into 2.5 cm (1 in) pieces
3 garlic cloves, crushed
2 cm (¾ in) piece ginger, finely grated
1 fresh or dried bay leaf
1 teaspoon dried chilli flakes (optional)
2 lemongrass stalks, pale section only, bruised
2 tablespoons fish sauce, plus extra to taste
500 ml (17 fl oz/2 cups) chicken stock
400 ml (13½ fl oz) tin coconut milk
2 potatoes, cut into 2.5 cm (1 in) pieces
1 small sweet potato, cut into 2.5 cm (1 in) pieces
1 teaspoon sugar, to taste
rice paddy herb or coriander (cilantro) leaves, chopped, to serve
crusty French bread or steamed rice, to serve

SERVES 4

Cut the chicken legs between the thighs and drumsticks. Using a heavy cleaver, cut each section in half again through the bone. You will have 16 pieces of chicken in total.

Combine the chicken pieces, garlic and onion powders, salt and 2 teaspoons of the curry powder in a large bowl.

Heat 2 tablespoons of the oil in a large heavy-based saucepan over medium–high heat. Working in batches, cook the chicken for 4–5 minutes per batch, until well browned all over. Transfer to a plate with a slotted spoon.

Add the onion, garlic and ginger to the pan, then reduce the heat to medium and cook, stirring, for 2–3 minutes, until the onion browns around the edges. Add the remaining curry powder, bay leaf, chilli flakes, if using, lemongrass, fish sauce, stock and half the coconut milk. Return the chicken to the pan, adding a little water if necessary, to just cover the chicken. Bring to the boil, then reduce the heat to a simmer and cook, covered, for 15 minutes. Add the potato, cook for 5 minutes, then add the sweet potato. Simmer, uncovered, for a further 15 minutes, or until the chicken, potato and sweet potato are cooked and the liquid is reduced and slightly thickened. Add the remaining coconut milk and return the mixture to a simmer. Season with a little freshly ground black pepper and add the sugar and extra fish sauce, to taste, if necessary.

Scatter the curry with the rice paddy herb or coriander and serve with French bread or steamed rice on the side.

Chicken jalfrezi
India

1 kg (2 lb 3 oz) skinless chicken thigh
  fillets, cut into 3 cm (1¼ in) chunks
1½ tablespoons ground cumin
1½ tablespoons ground coriander
1 tablespoon ground turmeric
80 ml (2½ fl oz/⅓ cup) vegetable oil
1 large onion, finely chopped
4 garlic cloves, crushed
4 cm (1½ in) piece ginger, finely grated
1 red capsicum (bell pepper), seeded
  and sliced
1 green capsicum (bell pepper), seeded and
  sliced
3 green chillies, finely chopped
4 large tomatoes, very finely chopped
  or puréed
½–1 teaspoon salt, to taste
2 teaspoons Garam masala (see page 218
  or use store-bought)
coriander (cilantro) leaves, chopped,
  to serve (optional)
steamed basmati rice (see page 178)
  or papadums, to serve

SERVES 4–6

Combine the chicken with the spices in a large bowl. Set aside for 10 minutes.

Heat the oil in a large heavy-based saucepan or flameproof casserole dish over high heat. Working in two batches, add the chicken and brown on all sides. Using a slotted spoon, transfer the chicken to a plate. Add the onion, garlic, ginger, capsicums and chilli to the pan and cook, stirring frequently, for 5 minutes, until the vegetables have softened.

Add the tomato and 250 ml (8½ fl oz/1 cup) water and simmer over low heat for 5 minutes. Add the chicken and simmer for a further 15–20 minutes, until the chicken is tender. Season with the salt and sprinkle in the garam masala.

Scatter the coriander over the top of the curry, if using, and serve with rice or papadums on the side.

Trinidadian duck curry
Trinidad & Tobago

To make the green seasoning, place the ingredients in the bowl of a small food processor and blend to a paste. Set aside.

To make the spice mix, lightly toast the spices in a dry frying pan over medium heat. Transfer to a mortar and pestle or spice grinder and grind to a powder.

Wash the duck in a bowl of cold running water with the flour. This will help remove any blood. Rinse and drain well. Pat dry with paper towel.

Place the duck in a bowl with the curry powders, salt, pepper, half the green seasoning and the spice mix. Mix well to combine, then set aside in the fridge to marinate for at least 4 hours.

To make the curry, heat the oil in a heavy-based saucepan or flameproof casserole dish over low heat. Add the onion and cook for 5 minutes. Add the pepper, garlic, curry leaves and cumin seeds and cook, stirring, for 2 minutes.

Combine the curry powders and 60 ml (2 fl oz/¼ cup) water in a small bowl. Add the liquid to the pan and stir for 2 minutes, until the mixture begins to clump together. Add the duck and increase the heat to high. Cook, stirring occasionally, for about 10 minutes, until the liquid has almost evaporated. Add the chilli, remaining green seasoning and boiling water. Cover, and simmer for 40 minutes, or until the duck is tender. Add the salt to taste and the coriander.

Serve with steamed rice or flatbreads on the side.

1.5 kg (3 lb 5 oz) duck legs (marylands)
plain (all-purpose) flour, for washing
2 teaspoons Madras curry powder
2 teaspoons hot curry powder
1 teaspoon salt
½ teaspoon freshly ground black pepper
steamed rice or flatbreads, to serve

Green seasoning
large handful coriander (cilantro) leaves
large handful flat leaf parsley leaves
½ celery stalk
4 garlic cloves, peeled
3 spring onions (scallions), trimmed
⅓ loosely packed cup thyme leaves
½ pimento or banana pepper, seeded

Spice mix
3 teaspoons coriander seeds
1 teaspoon cumin seeds
¼ teaspoon black peppercorns
¼ teaspoon fennel seeds
¼ teaspoon brown mustard seeds
¼ teaspoon fenugreek seeds

Curry
2 tablespoons vegetable oil
1 medium onion, sliced
4 pimento or banana peppers, thinly sliced
6 garlic cloves, finely chopped
10–12 curry leaves
½ teaspoon cumin seeds
1 tablespoon Madras curry powder
1 tablespoon duck/goat curry powder
1 hot chilli of choice, sliced
500 ml (17 fl oz/2 cups) boiling water
1 teaspoon salt, or to taste
handful chopped coriander (cilantro)
   leaves

SERVES 4

Hyderabadi chicken

8 x 150 g (5½ oz) chicken drumsticks or 1.2 kg (2 lb 10 oz) chicken thigh cutlets or fillets, cut into 3 cm (1¼ in) chunks

200 g (7 oz) plain yoghurt

1 teaspoon chilli powder

2 large onions, chopped

4 cm (1½ in) piece ginger, chopped

5 garlic cloves, peeled

50 g (1¾ oz/⅓ cup) raw cashew nuts or almonds

80 ml (2½ fl oz/⅓ cup) vegetable oil

1 tablespoon Garam masala (see page 218 or use store-bought)

3 tomatoes, puréed or very finely chopped

1 teaspoon ground turmeric

½ bunch coriander (cilantro), chopped, to serve

lemon wedges, to serve

Simple naan (see page 194), Paratha (see page 191) or steamed basmati rice (see page 178), to serve

SERVES 4–6

Combine the chicken, yoghurt, chilli powder and a pinch of salt in a large bowl. Set aside to marinate for at least 30 minutes.

Place the onion, ginger and garlic in a food processor and blend to a paste. Transfer to a bowl.

Blend the cashew nuts or almonds in the small bowl of a food processor with a splash of water to a paste.

Heat the oil in a large frying pan or heavy-based saucepan over medium heat. Add the onion paste and cook, stirring occasionally, for 5 minutes, or until soft.

Add the garam masala and cook, stirring, for 2 minutes. Add the tomato and turmeric and cook for a further 4–5 minutes, until the oil starts to separate.

Add the chicken and its marinade to the pan, along with the cashew nut paste and 125 ml (4 fl oz/½ cup) water. Stir to combine. Gently simmer for 15–20 minutes, until the chicken is tender. Season with salt, to taste.

Scatter the coriander over the top of the curry and serve with lemon wedges for squeezing over and naan, paratha or steamed basmati rice on the side.

Chicken karahi

Pakistan

80 ml (2½ fl oz/⅓ cup) vegetable oil

1 kg (2 lb 3 oz) skinless chicken thigh fillets, cut into 3 cm (1¼ in) cubes

4 cm (1½ in) piece ginger, finely grated, plus extra finely shredded to serve

6 garlic cloves, crushed

3 green chillies, seeded and finely chopped, plus extra thinly sliced to serve

1 teaspoon ground coriander

1 teaspoon ground cumin

1 teaspoon ground turmeric

½ teaspoon chilli powder

½ teaspoon freshly ground black pepper

1 teaspoon salt

4 medium tomatoes, finely chopped

125 g (4½ oz/½ cup) plain yoghurt

1 teaspoon Garam masala (see page 218 or use store-bought)

coriander (cilantro) leaves, to serve (optional)

lemon wedges, to serve

Simple naan (see page 194), to serve

SERVES 4

Heat the oil in a large frying pan with a lid or a heavy-based saucepan over high heat. Add the chicken and brown on all sides. Reduce the heat to medium, add the ginger, garlic and chilli and cook, stirring, for 2 minutes. Add the spices and salt and cook, stirring, for 1 minute, until fragrant.

Add the tomato, increase the heat and bring to the boil. Add the yoghurt, then reduce the heat to low and simmer, covered, for 15 minutes, or until the chicken is cooked through. Sprinkle over the garam masala.

Scatter over the coriander leaves, if using, along with the extra ginger and chilli. Serve with lemon wedges for squeezing over and naan bread on the side.

Pork & beef

Beef madras
India

Combine the ground coriander, cumin, chilli, turmeric, black pepper, mustard seeds, salt, garlic and ginger in a bowl with enough vinegar to form a paste.

Heat 2 tablespoons of the ghee in a heavy-based saucepan over medium heat. Add the spice paste and cook, stirring constantly, for 2–3 minutes, until fragrant. Using a spoon, carefully transfer the cooked spice paste to a large heatproof bowl, leaving any ghee behind.

Add the remaining ghee to the pan, along with the onion. Cook, stirring, for 3–4 minutes, until the onion is soft and golden. Using a slotted spoon, scoop out the onion and add it to the cooked spice paste.

Increase the heat to high. Working in batches, cook the beef, stirring, for 2–3 minutes, or until browned all over. Transfer to the bowl.

Return all the beef, onion and spices to the pan. Cook, stirring, for 1 minute, or until the meat is well-coated in the paste. Add the tomato and 125 ml (4 fl oz/½ cup) water, reduce the heat to medium and bring to the boil. Reduce the heat to low, cover and cook, stirring occasionally, for 1 hour 45 minutes, or until the beef is tender. Add a little extra water if the meat starts to stick to the base of the pan.

Remove the lid and cook, uncovered, for a further 15 minutes, or until the sauce has reduced and thickened slightly.

Serve with steamed basmati rice and yoghurt on the side and garnish with coriander sprigs, if you like.

2 tablespoons ground coriander

1 tablespoon ground cumin

2 teaspoons chilli powder

1 teaspoon ground turmeric

1 teaspoon freshly ground black pepper

1 teaspoon black mustard seeds

½ teaspoon salt

2 garlic cloves, crushed

2 cm (¾ in) piece ginger, finely grated

2–3 tablespoons white vinegar

3 tablespoons ghee

2 onions, sliced

1 kg (2 lb 3 oz) chuck steak or other stewing beef, cut into 2.5 cm (1 in) pieces

400 g (14 oz) tin crushed tomatoes

steamed basmati rice (see page 178), to serve

plain yoghurt, to serve

coriander (cilantro) sprigs, to garnish (optional)

SERVES 4

Beef rendang
Indonesia

3 tablespoons desiccated coconut

2 tablespoons vegetable oil

1 x quantity Rendang curry paste
(see page 212)

1.5 kg (3 lb 5 oz) chuck steak, oyster blade
or other stewing beef, cut into 3 cm
(1¼ in) pieces

400 ml (13½ fl oz) tin coconut milk

2 lemongrass stalks, pale section only,
bruised

6 kaffir lime leaves, torn

2 teaspoons tamarind purée

Roti canai (see page 199), to serve

SERVES 4–6

Toast the desiccated coconut in a large dry saucepan over medium heat, until golden. Transfer to a plate and set aside.

Heat the oil in the same saucepan over medium–low heat and add the curry paste. Cook, stirring constantly, for 3–4 minutes, until fragrant. Add the beef, coconut milk, lemongrass, lime leaves, tamarind and reserved toasted coconut, along with enough water to just cover the beef. Increase the heat to medium and bring to the boil. Reduce the heat to low and simmer, partially covered and stirring occasionally, for 1½–2 hours, until the sauce thickens and the beef is tender.

Remove the lid and simmer, uncovered, for 5–10 minutes, to thicken the sauce, if necessary. The curry should be fairly dry.

Serve with roti.

Goan pork sausage curry
India

300 g (10½ oz) Goan pork sausages (or use Portuguese chouriço)

2 tablespoons peanut (ground nut) oil, plus extra if necessary

2 potatoes (about 400 g/14 oz), cut into 1.5 cm (½ in) pieces

1 onion, sliced

2 cm (¾ in) piece ginger, finely grated

1 garlic clove, crushed

1 tablespoon tomato paste (concentrated purée)

3 tomatoes, chopped

1 small green capsicum (bell pepper), cut into 1.5 cm (½ in) pieces

1 long green chilli, sliced

lime pickle, to serve

4 soft white bread rolls, to serve

SERVES 4

Remove the sausage meat from its casings and coarsely crumble into 1.5–2 cm (½–¾ in) pieces. Place the meat in a large dry frying pan and place over medium heat. Cook, stirring occasionally, for 5–10 minutes, until the oil starts to release from the sausage meat and the meat browns. Using a slotted spoon, transfer the meat to a plate. Heat 1 tablespoon of the oil in the same pan and add the potato. Cook, stirring occasionally, for 3–4 minutes, until it starts to gain a bit of colour. Transfer the potato to the plate with the sausage.

Add the remaining oil to the pan, along with the onion, ginger and garlic and cook, stirring, for 2–3 minutes, until fragrant. Add the tomato paste and cook, stirring constantly, for 30 seconds, then add the tomatoes and 375 ml (12½ fl oz/1½ cups) water. Bring to the boil, return the sausage meat and potato to the pan and add the capsicum and chilli. Reduce the heat to a simmer and cook, covered, for 15–20 minutes, until the potato is tender and the mixture has thickened. (Add a little more water during cooking if the mixture starts to stick to the base of the pan.)

Serve with lime pickle and soft white bread rolls on the side.

Beef brisket curry
Hong Kong

1 kg (2 lb 3 oz) beef brisket, trimmed,
   cut into 3 cm (1¼ in) chunks

2 tablespoons peanut (ground nut) oil

1 red onion, thinly sliced

2.5 cm (1 in) piece ginger, thinly sliced

4 garlic cloves, finely chopped

2 pieces dried orange or tangerine peel,
   soaked in hot water for 10 minutes,
   drained

2 cinnamon sticks

3 whole star anise

2 dried bay leaves

1 teaspoon Chinese fivespice

70 g (2½ oz/¼ cup) Chu Hou paste

1 tablespoon light soy sauce

1 tablespoon oyster sauce

2 teaspoons dark soy sauce

2 tablespoons chopped rock sugar

2 tablespoons Shaoxing rice wine

500 ml (17 fl oz/2 cups) chicken stock

1 medium carrot, thickly sliced diagonally

½ daikon (white radish), cut into
   large chunks

steamed jasmine rice (see page 178),
   to serve

sliced spring onions (scallions), to serve

coriander (cilantro) leaves, to serve

SERVES 4

Bring a large saucepan of water to the boil. Add the beef and blanch for 3–4 minutes, until it comes back to the boil. Using a slotted spoon, remove the beef and transfer to a bowl or plate.

Heat the oil in a heavy-based saucepan or flameproof casserole dish over medium heat. Add the onion, ginger, garlic, orange peel, cinnamon, star anise, bay leaves and Chinese fivespice and cook, stirring, for 3–4 minutes, until the onion has softened. Increase the heat to high, add the beef and gently sear, being careful not to burn the spices.

Add the Chu Hou paste, light soy sauce, oyster sauce, dark soy sauce and sugar and cook for 1 minute. Add the Shaoxing rice wine and chicken stock and bring to the boil. Reduce the heat to low, cover and cook for 2 hours. Add the carrot and daikon and cook for 20 minutes, or until the vegetables have softened and the beef is very tender. Simmer, uncovered, for a few extra minutes, if you prefer a slightly thicker sauce.

Divide the rice among plates, spoon the curry over the top and scatter with sliced spring onion and coriander leaves.

Japanese beef curry
Japan

1 tablespoon peanut (ground nut) or
   vegetable oil, plus extra if necessary
400 g (14 oz) beef rump steak, cut into
   thin strips or 1.5 cm (½ in) chunks
2 onions, thinly sliced
1 tablespoon tomato paste (concentrated
   purée)
2 carrots or 1 sweet potato, cut into
   1.5 cm (½ in) chunks
1 potato, cut into 1.5 cm (½ in) chunks
1 apple, peeled, cored and sliced
100 g (3½ oz) Japanese curry sauce mix
   (curry roux blocks) (see notes)
60 g (2 oz/½ cup) frozen peas, thawed
2 teaspoons worcestershire or soy sauce
steamed sticky rice, to serve

SERVES 4

Heat the oil in a large heavy-based saucepan over high heat. Working in batches, add the beef and cook for 1–2 minutes, adding a little more oil between batches if necessary, until the meat is browned but not cooked through. Transfer to a plate with a slotted spoon and reduce the heat to medium–low. Add the onion and a little more oil to the pan if needed and cook for 5–6 minutes, until soft and lightly browned. Add the tomato paste and cook, stirring, for 1 minute.

Add the carrot or sweet potato, potato, apple and 750 ml (25½ fl oz/3 cups) water and mix well. Increase the heat and bring to the boil, then reduce the heat to medium–low and simmer, covered, for 15–20 minutes, until the vegetables are just tender. Crumble the sauce mix cubes into the pan and stir until dissolved and combined. Return the beef to the mixture and stir in the peas and worcestershire or soy sauce. Simmer for 2–3 minutes, stirring constantly, until the beef is cooked through.

Serve with steamed sticky rice.

NOTES: JAPANESE CURRY SAUCE MIX CAN BE PURCHASED FROM MOST SUPERMARKETS IN THE INTERNATIONAL AISLE OR FROM ASIAN AND JAPANESE GROCERY STORES.

THIS CURRY IS ALSO GREAT MADE WITH DICED CHICKEN THIGH FILLETS AS AN ALTERNATIVE TO BEEF.

Beef massaman
Thailand

3 tablespoons peanut (ground nut) oil

1 kg (2 lb 3 oz) beef chuck steak or other stewing beef, cut into 2.5 cm (1 in) chunks

1 x 400 ml (13½ fl oz) tin coconut cream (do not shake before opening)

70 g (2½ oz/¼ cup) Massaman curry paste, (see page 209)

1 onion, cut into wedges

3 cm (1¼ in) piece ginger, julienned

2 tablespoons grated palm sugar, plus extra to taste

3 kaffir lime leaves, torn

1 tablespoon fish sauce, plus extra to taste

1 tablespoon tamarind purée, plus extra to taste

70 g (2½ oz/½ cup) raw peanuts

1 sweet potato, cut into 2 cm (¾ in) chunks

300 g (10½ oz) daikon (white radish), cut into matchsticks

Thai basil leaves, to serve

steamed jasmine rice (see page 178), to serve

SERVES 4

Heat 2 tablespoons of the peanut oil in a large heavy-based saucepan over high heat. Working in batches, add the beef and cook for 2–3 minutes, until browned all over. Transfer to a plate and set aside.

Reduce the heat to medium, scoop 2 tablespoons of the thick cream from the top of the coconut cream tin and add to the same saucepan with the remaining oil and cook until bubbling. Add the curry paste and cook, stirring constantly, for 2–3 minutes, until aromatic.

Add the onion and ginger and cook, stirring frequently, for 3–4 minutes, until the onion is lightly browned. Stir in the sugar, lime leaves, remaining coconut cream, fish sauce and tamarind. Return the beef to the pan and add just enough water to cover the beef. Bring to the boil, then reduce the heat to a simmer and cook, covered, for 1½ hours, or until the beef is almost tender.

Meanwhile, toast the peanuts in a large dry frying pan over medium heat, stirring frequently, for 3–4 minutes, until the skins loosen and the peanuts become fragrant and lightly browned in spots. Set aside to cool slightly, then rub off and discard the skins.

Add the sweet potato and most of the peanuts to the curry mixture, saving some for serving. Cook, uncovered, for a further 15–20 minutes, until the beef and potato are very tender and the sauce is slightly thickened. Stir in the daikon and cook for 1–2 minutes, until heated through.

Season to taste with extra palm sugar, fish sauce and tamarind purée to balance the flavour, if necessary.

Scatter the curry with basil leaves and the reserved peanuts, and serve with jasmine rice on the side.

Pork vindaloo

India

1 kg (2 lb 3 oz) pork scotch fillet (neck) or other stewing pork, cut into 3 cm (1¼ in) pieces
1 x quantity Vindaloo curry paste (see page 217)
125 ml (4 fl oz/½ cup) coconut vinegar or 2 tablespoons white vinegar
3 tablespoons ghee or vegetable oil
1 teaspoon black mustard seeds
1 sprig curry leaves
2 onions, finely chopped
2 tomatoes, finely chopped
1 fresh or dried bay leaf (preferably Indian)
1 teaspoon salt
steamed basmati rice (see page 178), to serve

SERVES   4

Combine the pork, curry paste and vinegar in a large bowl. Cover, refrigerate and marinate for at least 2 hours or overnight.

Heat the ghee in a large heavy-based saucepan over medium heat. Add the mustard seeds and curry leaves and sizzle for a few seconds. When the seeds start to crackle, add the onion, then reduce the heat to medium–low and cook, stirring occasionally, for 10–12 minutes, until the onion is golden brown. Add the tomato, bay leaf and the pork with its marinade to the pan. Stir well and add just enough water to cover.

Bring to the boil, then reduce the heat to low, cover and cook, stirring occasionally, for 1–1½ hours, until the meat is tender and the sauce has thickened slightly. If necessary, remove the lid and continue to cook, uncovered, for a further 15–20 minutes, to reduce the sauce to the desired consistency. Season with the salt.

Serve with steamed basmati rice.

Pepper beef curry
Sri Lanka

4 teaspoons black peppercorns

1 tablespoon coriander seeds

2 teaspoons cumin seeds

1 teaspoon salt

½ teaspoon ground turmeric

1 kg (2 lb 3 oz) beef chuck steak or other stewing beef, cut into 5 cm (2 in) chunks

2 onions, chopped

4 small green chillies, halved lengthways

3 garlic cloves, crushed

2 cm (¾ in) piece ginger, finely grated

1 sprig curry leaves

20 cm (8 in) length pandan leaf, tied in a knot

1 lemongrass stalk, pale section only, bruised

2 tablespoons white vinegar

400 ml (13½ fl oz) tin coconut milk

2 tablespoons ghee or vegetable oil

½ teaspoon ground fennel

125 ml (4 fl oz/½ cup) coconut cream

coriander (cilantro) leaves, to serve

steamed rice, to serve

lime wedges, to serve

SERVES 4

Toast the peppercorns, coriander and cumin seeds separately in a small dry frying pan for 30 seconds, or until fragrant. Grind in a spice grinder or mortar and pestle to a fine powder.

Toss the freshly ground spices, salt and turmeric with the beef in a medium heavy-based saucepan. Set aside to marinate for 30 minutes.

Add the onion, chilli, garlic, ginger, curry leaves, pandan leaf, lemongrass, vinegar and coconut milk to the marinated beef. Slowly bring to the boil over medium–low heat, then reduce the heat slightly and simmer, covered, for 1½–2 hours, until the meat is tender.

Strain the beef and reserve the juices and aromatics. Add the ghee or oil to the saucepan and heat over high heat. Return the cooked beef to the pan and fry for 5–6 minutes, until lightly browned. Return the reserved juices and aromatics to the pan and add the fennel and coconut cream. Bring to the boil over medium heat and simmer, uncovered, for 15–20 minutes, until the meat is very tender and the sauce has thickened slightly.

Scatter a few coriander leaves over the top of the curry and serve with steamed rice and lime wedges for squeezing over.

600 g (1 lb 5 oz) thick pork sausages

2 tablespoons peanut (ground nut) oil

2 onions, thinly sliced

2 tablespoons all-purpose curry powder

400 g (14 oz) tin diced tomatoes

250 ml (8½ fl oz/1 cup) beef stock

1 teaspoon soy or worcestershire sauce

130 g (4½ oz/1 cup) frozen baby peas

55 g (2 oz/⅓ cup) sultanas (golden raisins)

1 granny smith apple, cored, quartered
and thinly sliced

mashed potato, to serve

fruit chutney, to serve

SERVES 4

Curried pork sausages
Australia

Place the sausages in large saucepan and add enough cold water to cover. Bring to the boil over high heat, then reduce the heat to a simmer and cook for 2 minutes. Drain the sausages and leave to cool slightly, then thickly slice diagonally.

Heat 1 tablespoon of the oil in a large frying pan over medium heat. Add the sausage pieces and cook, stirring occasionally, for 3–4 minutes, until lightly browned. Using a slotted spoon, transfer to a plate and set aside. Add the remaining oil and the onion to the pan and cook, stirring occasionally, for 4–5 minutes, until soft. Add the curry powder and cook, stirring, for 1 minute, or until fragrant.

Return the sliced sausage to the pan, stir to coat in the curry mixture, then add the tomato, stock and soy or worcestershire sauce. Simmer, uncovered, for about 5 minutes, or until thickened slightly. Stir in the peas and sultanas and cook for a further 5 minutes, then stir through the apple.

Serve with mashed potato and fruit chutney on the side.

Korean-style curry rice
South Korea

1 tablespoon sesame oil

1 tablespoon peanut (ground nut) or vegetable oil

400 g (14 oz) boneless beef short ribs, cut into 1.5 cm (½ in) chunks

1 onion, roughly chopped

2 carrots, cut into 1.5 cm (½ in) chunks

1 potato, cut into 1.5 cm (½ in) chunks

100 g (3½ oz) packet Korean curry powder (see notes)

100 g (3½ oz) cauliflower florets

100 g (3½ oz) button mushrooms, halved or quartered depending on size

steamed rice, to serve

kimchi, to serve

SERVES 4

Heat the oils in a large heavy-based saucepan over medium–high heat. Working in two batches, add the beef and cook for 4–5 minutes, until well browned all over. Transfer to a plate using a slotted spoon. Add the onion to the pan and cook for 2–3 minutes, until brown around the edges.

Return the beef to the pan and add the carrot, potato, curry powder and 750 ml (25½ fl oz/3 cups) water and mix well. Bring to the boil, then reduce the heat to medium–low and simmer, covered, for 5 minutes. Add the cauliflower and mushroom and simmer, covered, for a further 10–15 minutes or until the beef and vegetables are tender.

Serve with steamed rice and kimchi on the side.

NOTES: KOREAN CURRY POWDER CAN BE PURCHASED FROM ASIAN OR KOREAN GROCERY STORES OR ONLINE. YOU CAN CHOOSE BETWEEN MILD, MEDIUM OR HOT CURRY POWDER.

THIS CURRY IS GREAT MADE WITH DICED CHICKEN THIGH FILLETS AS AN ALTERNATIVE TO BEEF.

Pork & peanut curry
Thailand

Place the pork in a large saucepan and cover with water. Bring to the boil over medium heat, stirring occasionally. Once the water starts to boil, remove from the heat and drain the pork. Toast the peanuts in a large dry frying pan over medium heat, stirring often, for 3–4 minutes, until the skins loosen and the peanuts become fragrant and lightly browned in spots. Set aside to cool slightly, then rub off the skins with a clean tea towel and discard.

Heat the 2 tablespoons of oil in a wok or large saucepan and cook the grated ginger and garlic for 1 minute. Add the curry paste, onion and blanched pork and cook, stirring, for 3–4 minutes, until fragrant. Add the sugar, fish sauce, star anise and toasted peanuts. Cook, stirring, for a further 2–3 minutes, until the mixture starts to stick to the base of the pan. Add the tamarind and enough water to cover the pork by about 1 cm (½ in). Bring to the boil, then reduce the heat to low and simmer, uncovered, for 1¼–1½ hours, until the pork is very tender. Add a little extra water if the meat starts to stick. Using a slotted spoon, transfer the pork to a colander and drain well over a bowl, returning any sauce to the pan. Set the pork aside to dry in a single layer.

Heat enough peanut oil for deep-frying in a medium saucepan to 170°C (340°F). Working in batches, fry the pork for about 2 minutes per batch, until well browned. Drain on paper towel.

Reheat the sauce over medium heat, return the pork to the pan and season to taste with extra palm sugar, fish sauce and tamarind purée. Scatter the curry with coriander and the julienned ginger, and serve with steamed jasmine rice.

1 kg (2 lb 3 oz) boneless pork belly with skin, cut into 2 cm (¾ in) pieces

80 g (2¾ oz/½ cup) raw peanuts

2 tablespoons peanut (ground nut) oil, plus extra to deep-fry

4 cm (1½ in) piece ginger, finely grated, plus extra, julienned, to serve

2 garlic cloves, crushed

120 g (4½ oz/⅓ cup) Green curry paste (see page 207)

1 large red onion, roughly chopped

2 tablespoons grated palm sugar, plus extra to taste

2 tablespoons fish sauce, plus extra to taste

1 whole star anise

2 tablespoons tamarind purée, plus extra to taste

coriander (cilantro) sprigs, to serve

steamed jasmine rice (see page 178), to serve

SERVES 4–6

Saraman curry
Cambodia

2 tablespoons peanut (ground nut) oil

1.2 kg (2 lb 10 oz) beef chuck steak or other stewing beef, trimmed and cut into large chunks

250 ml (8½ fl oz/1 cup) coconut cream

500 ml (17 fl oz/2 cups) coconut milk

70 g (2½ oz/½ cup) unsalted roasted peanuts

1½ tablespoons grated palm sugar, or to taste

1½ tablespoons fish sauce, or to taste

1½ tablespoons tamarind purée, or to taste

thinly sliced red onion, to serve

thinly sliced long red chillies, to serve

steamed jasmine rice (see page 178) and Roti canai (see page 199), to serve

Spice paste

3 teaspoons coriander seeds

1 teaspoon cumin seeds

3 whole star anise

3 whole cloves

4 cardamom pods, bruised and seeds removed

1 small cinnamon stick, broken

3 dried red chillies, seeded, soaked in hot water for 15 minutes, drained

2 lemongrass stalks, pale section only, chopped

3 Asian shallots or 1 red onion, chopped

6 garlic cloves, peeled

1 teaspoon finely chopped galangal

1 teaspoon grated ginger

1 kaffir lime leaf, torn

3 coriander (cilantro) roots, scraped

1 teaspoon finely grated turmeric

1 teaspoon shrimp paste

1 teaspoon salt

75 g (2½ oz) freshly grated coconut, toasted

SERVES 4

To make the paste, place the coriander and cumin seeds, star anise, cloves, cardamom seeds and cinnamon stick in a small dry frying pan and toast for 1–2 minutes, until fragrant. Set aside to cool.

Place the chillies, lemongrass, shallot, garlic, galangal, ginger, lime leaf, coriander roots and turmeric in a large mortar and pestle or the bowl of a food processor and pound or blitz until finely chopped. Add the toasted spices, shrimp paste and salt. Pound or blitz again until a smooth paste forms. Stir through the coconut.

Heat the oil in a large heavy-based saucepan over medium heat. Add the spice paste and cook, stirring constantly, for 2–3 minutes, until fragrant. Increase the heat to high, add the beef and sear on all sides.

Add the coconut cream and milk and bring just to the boil, then reduce the heat to low and simmer, covered, for 1½ hours. The beef must stay covered by the sauce throughout cooking, so add a little water if the sauce evaporates too much.

Add the peanuts, palm sugar, fish sauce and tamarind purée. Simmer for a further 20–30 minutes, until the beef is completely tender. Adjust the seasoning with more palm sugar, fish sauce and tamarind, if necessary.

Scatter the red onion and sliced chilli over the top and serve with steamed rice and roti.

Myanmar pork curry
Myanmar

1 kg (2 lb 3 oz) boneless pork belly, cut into 2.5–3 cm (1–1¼ in) chunks

1 teaspoon ground turmeric

2 tablespoons fish sauce, plus extra to taste

1 teaspoon chilli powder

1 teaspoon paprika

¼ teaspoon black pepper

80 ml (2½ fl oz/⅓ cup) peanut (ground nut) oil

6 garlic cloves, crushed

5 cm (2 in) piece ginger, finely grated

4 Asian shallots or 2 medium red onions, finely chopped

1 lemongrass stalk, pale section only, bruised (optional)

2 teaspoons sugar

juice of 1 lime

coriander (cilantro) leaves, to serve

steamed jasmine rice (see page 178), to serve

SERVES 4

Combine the pork belly, turmeric, fish sauce, chilli powder, paprika and pepper in a large bowl. Set aside to marinate for 1 hour.

Heat half the oil in a large heavy-based saucepan until hot. Working in two batches, add the pork and cook, turning frequently, until browned all over. Remove the pork from the pan and set aside on a plate. Reduce the heat to low, add the remaining oil to the pan and cook the garlic, ginger and shallot for 5 minutes.

Return the pork to the pan, add the lemongrass (if using) and 500–625 ml (17–21 fl oz/2–2½ cups) water. Cover and cook over low heat for 1½ hours, or until the pork is tender. Stir in the sugar, season to taste with more fish sauce, if required, and stir through the lime juice.

Scatter with coriander and serve with steamed jasmine rice on the side.

80 ml (2½ fl oz/⅓ cup) vegetable oil

2 onions, finely chopped

5 garlic cloves, finely chopped

4 cm (1½ in) piece ginger, finely grated

4 cardamom pods, bruised and seeds removed

4 whole cloves

2 cinnamon sticks

2 teaspoons ground cumin

2 teaspoons ground coriander

1½ teaspoons ground turmeric

1 teaspoon chilli powder

½ teaspoon mustard seeds

¼ teaspoon freshly ground black pepper

3 fresh or dried bay leaves

1 kg (2 lb 3 oz) beef chuck steak or other stewing beef, trimmed, cut into 3 cm (1¼ in) pieces

1 teaspoon sugar, or to taste

1 teaspoon salt, or to taste

chopped mint or coriander (cilantro) leaves, to serve

steamed basmati rice (see page 178) or Simple naan (see page 194), to serve

SERVES 4

Bengali beef curry
India

Heat the oil in a large frying pan or heavy-based saucepan over low heat. Add the onion and cook for 15 minutes, or until just golden and very soft. Add the garlic, ginger, spices and bay leaves. Add 125 ml (4 fl oz/½ cup) water and simmer until the water has almost evaporated.

Add the beef and 250 ml (8½ fl oz/1 cup) water. Cover and cook for 45 minutes, then add another 125 ml (4 fl oz/½ cup) water and simmer, covered, for a further 45 minutes, or until the beef is very tender. (Keep adding water if necessary to maintain a saucy consistency.) Add the sugar and salt, to taste.

Scatter the herbs over the curry and serve with steamed basmati rice or naan.

Lamb & goat

Kerala lamb
South India

1 kg (2 lb 3 oz) boneless lamb shoulder or
    other stewing lamb, cut into 2.5 cm
    (1 in) pieces
1 tablespoon coconut oil
80 g (2¾ oz) thinly sliced fresh coconut
½ teaspoon black mustard seeds
2 sprigs curry leaves
1 large onion, thinly sliced
2 long green chillies, sliced
3 cm (1¼ in) piece ginger, julienned
3 garlic cloves, sliced
2 tomatoes, chopped
2 teaspoons sweet paprika
steamed basmati rice (see page 178) and
    Simple naan (see page 194), to serve

Marinade
4 dried red chillies
2 cm (¾ in) piece cinnamon stick
1½ teaspoons coriander seeds
½ teaspoon cumin seeds
½ teaspoon fennel seeds
½ teaspoon black peppercorns
2 cloves
½ teaspoon ground turmeric
1 garlic clove, crushed
1 cm (½ in) piece ginger, finely grated
1 long green chilli, sliced
2 teaspoons white vinegar

SERVES 4

To make the marinade, roast the whole spices separately in a dry frying pan over medium heat for 30 seconds, or until fragrant. Grind in a spice grinder or mortar and pestle to a fine powder.

Combine the lamb, roasted spices and the remaining marinade ingredients in a large bowl. Cover, then refrigerate and marinate for 2 hours or overnight.

Heat the coconut oil in a large heavy-based frying pan over medium–high heat. Add the coconut and cook, stirring, for 1–2 minutes, until lightly toasted. Transfer to a plate using a slotted spoon. Add the mustard seeds and curry leaves to the pan and sizzle for a few seconds. When the seeds start to crackle, add the onion, chilli, ginger and garlic. Reduce the heat to medium–low and cook, stirring occasionally, for 12–15 minutes, until the onion is golden. Add the tomato and paprika and cook for 8–10 minutes or until the tomato breaks down.

Add the lamb with its marinade to the tomato mixture. Stir well and add just enough water to cover. Bring to the boil, then reduce the heat to low. Add most of the toasted coconut (reserving some for garnish), then cover and cook, stirring occasionally, for 1½–2 hours, until the lamb is tender and the sauce has reduced and thickened slightly. If the liquid is still watery, remove the lid and continue to cook for a further 15–20 minutes.

Scatter with the reserved coconut and serve with steamed basmati rice and naan.

Caribbean goat curry
Jamaica

3 tablespoons all-purpose curry powder

1 teaspoon allspice berries

3–4 tablespoons vegetable oil

1.5 kg (3 lb 5 oz) bone-in goat casserole meat (cut into 3–4 cm/1¼–1½ in pieces by your butcher)

1 onion, roughly chopped

3 tablespoons tomato paste (concentrated purée)

4 garlic cloves, crushed

3 cm (1¼ in) piece ginger, finely grated

1 teaspoon ground white pepper

2 fresh thyme sprigs

1–2 scotch bonnet or other hot chillies (seeded if you prefer less heat), sliced

750 ml (25½ fl oz/3 cups) lamb or chicken stock

2 potatoes, cut into 2.5 cm (1 in) chunks

coriander (cilantro) leaves, to serve

steamed rice and Roti canai (see page 199), to serve

SERVES 4

Toast the curry powder and allspice in a small dry frying pan over medium heat, shaking the pan constantly, for 1–2 minutes, until fragrant and slightly darkened in colour.

Heat 2 tablespoons of the oil in a large heavy-based saucepan over medium–high heat. Working in batches, cook the goat, turning frequently, for 4–5 minutes, until well browned all over. Transfer to a plate using a slotted spoon. Add a little more oil to the pan between batches if necessary.

Add the onion to the pan, then reduce the heat to medium and cook for 2–3 minutes, until the onion browns around the edges. Add the tomato paste, garlic, ginger, white pepper and roasted curry powder mixture and cook, stirring continuously, for 1 minute. Return the goat to the pan, add the thyme and chilli and pour over the stock to just cover the goat. Add a little extra water if necessary.

Bring to the boil, then reduce the heat to a simmer and cook, covered, for 1½ hours, or until the goat is just tender. Add the potato and simmer, uncovered, for 15–20 minutes, until the potato is tender and the liquid is reduced slightly and a little thickened. Allow the potato to break down slightly to thicken the sauce further if you like.

Scatter the curry with coriander and serve with steamed rice and roti.

60 ml (2 fl oz/¼ cup) vegetable oil

1 large onion, finely chopped

2 cinnamon sticks

4 cardamom pods, smashed

4 whole cloves

1 teaspoon fennel seeds

6 fresh curry leaves

2 fresh or dried bay leaves

4 garlic cloves, finely chopped

4 cm (1¼ in) piece ginger, finely grated

1 teaspoon ground turmeric

500 g (1 lb 2 oz) tomatoes, blended to
    a purée or finely chopped

1.1–1.2 kg (2 lb 7 oz–2 lb 10 oz) boneless
    lamb shoulder, trimmed and chopped
    into 3 cm (1¼ in) chunks

400 g (14 oz) potatoes, diced

1 teaspoon Garam masala (see
    page 218 or use store-bought),
    or to taste

½ teaspoon salt, or to taste

1–2 teaspoons sugar, to taste

1 unsliced white sandwich loaf, cut
    into quarters

grated carrot, to serve

coriander (cilantro) leaves, to serve

Durban masala

1 teaspoon chilli powder

½ teaspoon ground coriander

½ teaspoon ground cumin

¼ teaspoon ground cardamom

¼ teaspoon cinnamon

¼ teaspoon ground ginger

⅛ teaspoon ground cloves

⅛ teaspoon ground mace

SERVES 4

Bunny chow
South Africa

To make the Durban masala, combine the ingredients in a small bowl. Set aside.

Heat the oil in a large heavy-based frying pan with a lid or heavy-based saucepan over medium heat. Add the onion, cinnamon, cardamom, cloves, fennel seeds, curry leaves and bay leaves and cook for 1 minute. Add the garlic, ginger, turmeric and Durban masala and cook, stirring, for 2 minutes. Stir in the tomato and 60 ml (2 fl oz/¼ cup) water and simmer for 2 minutes. Add the lamb and stir to coat in the mixture. Cover and simmer for 1¼–1½ hours, or until the lamb is tender. Add the potato and simmer for a further 15 minutes, or until tender. Season with the garam masala, salt and sugar to taste.

Remove most of the centre of each bread quarter in one large piece, leaving a 2 cm (¾ in) thick base. Set the bread centres aside. Fill each of the bread cases generously with the lamb curry.

Serve with grated carrot and coriander on the side and with the scooped-out bread pieces for dipping into the sauce.

Lamb massaman
Thailand

45 g (1½ oz/⅓ cup) unsalted roasted peanuts

3 tablespoons peanut (ground nut) oil

600 g (1 lb 5 oz) lamb backstrap loin, cut into 2 cm (¾ in) pieces

270 ml (9 fl oz) tin coconut cream (do not shake before opening)

3 tablespoons Massaman curry paste (see page 209)

250 g (9 oz) fresh pineapple, peeled and cut into 2 cm (¾ in) pieces

1 large desiree (or other waxy) potato, cut into 1.5 cm (½ in) pieces

2 tablespoons grated palm sugar, plus extra to taste

3 kaffir lime leaves, torn

250 ml (8½ fl oz/1 cup) chicken stock

1 tablespoon fish sauce, plus extra to taste

2 teaspoons tamarind purée, plus extra to taste

Thai basil leaves, to serve

steamed jasmine rice (see page 178), to serve

SERVES 4

Toast the peanuts in a large dry frying pan over medium heat, until they take on some colour. Remove from the pan and set aside to cool. Roughly chop the peanuts.

Heat 2 tablespoons of the oil in a large heavy-based saucepan over high heat. Working in batches, cook the lamb for 2–3 minutes or until well-browned all over, but not cooked through. Transfer to a plate and set aside.

Reduce the heat to medium, scoop 2 tablespoons of the thick cream from the top of the coconut cream tin and add to the same saucepan. Add the remaining oil and cook until bubbling. Add the curry paste and cook, stirring continuously, for 2–3 minutes, until aromatic.

Add the pineapple, potato and sugar and cook, stirring, for 2–3 minutes, until starting to caramelise. Add the lime leaves, remaining coconut cream, stock, fish sauce, tamarind, most of the peanuts (reserving some for garnish) and just enough water, if necessary, to cover the potato and pineapple.

Bring to the boil, then reduce the heat and simmer, covered, for 15–20 minutes, until the potato is tender and the sauce is reduced slightly. Return the lamb to the pan and cook, stirring, for 2–3 minutes, until the lamb is just cooked through.

Season to taste with extra fish sauce, palm sugar and tamarind to balance the flavour, if necessary.

Scatter the curry with basil leaves and the remaining peanuts and serve with steamed jasmine rice.

North African goat curry
Morocco

2 tablespoons olive oil

1–1.2 kg (2 lb 3 oz–2 lb 10 oz) bone-in goat shoulder (see note)

2 medium onions, finely chopped

3 garlic cloves, finely chopped

1 teaspoon ground cumin

1 teaspoon ground coriander

1 teaspoon ground turmeric

1 teaspoon paprika

1 teaspoon ground ginger

1 teaspoon ground cinnamon

½ teaspoon black pepper

½ teaspoon ground cardamom

¼ teaspoon ground nutmeg

¼ teaspoon ground cloves

2 teaspoons honey, to taste

½–1 teaspoon salt

170 g (6 oz) prunes, raisins or dates, soaked in boiling water until soft (optional)

Roti canai (see page 199), to serve

lemon wedges, to serve

Tomato, onion & parsley salad

6 tomatoes, sliced into wedges

1 white or red onion, thinly sliced

large handful flat-leaf parsley leaves, chopped

juice of ½ lemon

2 tablespoons olive oil

SERVES 4

To make the salad, combine the tomato, onion and parsley in a bowl. Season generously with salt and freshly ground black pepper and drizzle over the lemon juice and olive oil. Toss to combine and set aside for the flavours to infuse.

Heat the oil in a large heavy-based saucepan or flameproof casserole dish over medium heat. Brown the goat on both sides, then remove to a plate. Reduce the heat to low and add the onion and garlic. Cook, stirring occasionally, for 5 minutes. Add the spices and cook, stirring, for 1 minute.

Return the goat to the pan and pour in 375 ml (12½ fl oz/1½ cups) water. Cover and simmer for 45–50 minutes, until the goat is tender. Add the honey and season to taste with the salt. Add the prunes, raisins or dates, if using, and stir through. Gently remove the meat from the bones and discard the bones. The curry is now ready to serve, but if you prefer a thicker sauce, reduce the sauce further over medium heat.

Serve with roti and the salad on the side, and with lemon wedges for squeezing over.

NOTE: IF YOU LIKE, ASK YOUR BUTCHER TO CUT THE GOAT SHOULDER IN HALF TO MAKE IT EASIER TO COOK.

Cape Malay mutton curry
South Africa

60 ml (2 fl oz/¼ cup) vegetable oil

2 medium onions, finely chopped

4 garlic cloves, crushed

4 cm (1½ in) piece ginger, peeled and finely grated

3 whole cardamom pods, bruised

2 small or 1 large cinnamon stick

3 whole cloves

1.1 kg (2 lb 7 oz) boneless mutton or lamb shoulder, cut into 3 cm (1¼ in) chunks

1 tablespoon Cape Malay curry powder, roasted masala powder or meat curry powder

2 teaspoons ground coriander

1 teaspoon ground cumin

1 teaspoon ground turmeric

½ teaspoon chilli powder

2 medium tomatoes, finely chopped

3 medium or 2 large potatoes, cut into small chunks

180 g (6½ oz) dried apricots, soaked in boiling water for 10 minutes to soften (see note)

1 teaspoon salt, or to taste

½ teaspoon sugar, or to taste

lemon juice, to taste

chopped coriander (cilantro) leaves, to serve

steamed rice or Roti canai (see page 199), to serve

SERVES 4–6

Heat the oil in a large heavy-based saucepan or flameproof casserole dish over high heat. Add the onion, garlic and ginger, then reduce the heat to medium and cook, stirring occasionally, for 5 minutes, or until the onion has just softened. Increase the heat to high and add the cardamom, cinnamon, cloves and mutton or lamb. Stir until the meat is browned on all sides.

Stir in the curry powder and spices and cook for 1 minute. Add the tomato and 500 ml (17 fl oz/2 cups) water. Bring to the boil, then reduce the heat to low and cook, covered, for 1½ hours.

Add the potato and apricots and simmer, covered, for a further 15–20 minutes until the potato is tender. Season to taste with the salt, sugar and a squeeze of lemon juice, and scatter over the chopped coriander.

Serve with steamed rice or roti.

NOTE: THE SWEETNESS OF THE APRICOTS IN THIS DISH HELPS TO BALANCE THE SAVOURY FLAVOUR OF THE MUTTON. YOU CAN ALSO USE RAISINS OR 1 TABLESPOON APRICOT JAM INSTEAD.

3 tablespoons ghee

1 kg (2 lb 3 oz) boneless lamb shoulder,
cut into 5 cm (2 in) pieces

75 g (2½ oz/½ cup) raw cashew nuts

1 onion, roughly chopped

5 cm (2 in) piece ginger, coarsely chopped

3 garlic cloves, coarsely chopped

1 cinnamon stick

1 tablespoon ground coriander

2 teaspoons ground cumin

1 teaspoon cardamom pods, bruised

½ teaspoon ground Kashmiri chilli
powder, or to taste

250 g (9 oz/1 cup) plain yoghurt, plus extra
to serve

steamed basmati rice (see page 178),
to serve

SERVES 4

Lamb korma

Heat 1 tablespoon of the ghee in a large heavy-based saucepan over high heat. Season the lamb well with salt and pepper then, working in batches, add to pan and cook, turning frequently, for 5–7 minutes, until brown all over. Transfer to a plate.

Meanwhile, process the cashew nuts in a food processor or blender until finely chopped. Transfer to a bowl and set aside. Add the onion, ginger and garlic to the processor and blitz until puréed, adding a little water to get the mixture moving if needed.

Heat the remaining ghee in the pan over medium heat. Add the onion mixture and cook, stirring, for 10–15 minutes, until starting to caramelise. Increase the heat to medium–high, add the spices and cook, stirring continuously, for 3–4 minutes, until fragrant. Return the lamb to the pan, along with the ground cashew nuts and stir to coat the lamb. Add just enough water to cover the meat, then season and bring to the boil. Reduce the heat to low and simmer, half-covered and stirring occasionally, for 1½–2 hours, until the lamb is very tender and the sauce is reduced to just cover the meat. Add a splash of water if the mixture is drying out.

Stir in the yoghurt and return to the boil, then reduce the heat and simmer over very low heat, uncovered, for 10–15 minutes, until the sauce is thickened.

Serve with steamed basmati rice and extra yoghurt on the side.

Rogan josh

India

1 kg (2 lb 3 oz) boneless lamb shoulder or
leg, cut into 2.5 cm (1 in) pieces

375 g (13 oz/1½ cups) plain yoghurt

1 teaspoon salt

60 g (2 oz) ghee

1 cinnamon stick

2 teaspoons green cardamom pods, bruised

4 brown or black cardamom pods, bruised

½ teaspoon whole cloves

3 onions, chopped

5 cm (2 in) piece ginger, finely grated

4 garlic cloves, crushed

1 tablespoon Kashmiri chilli powder

2 teaspoons sweet paprika

2 teaspoons ground turmeric

large handful coriander (cilantro), chopped

1 teaspoon Garam masala (see page 218
or use store-bought)

Paratha (see page 191), to serve

SERVES 4

Combine the lamb, yoghurt and ½ teaspoon of the salt in a large bowl. Cover and set aside to marinate.

Heat the ghee in a heavy-based saucepan over medium heat. Add the cinnamon, cardamom and cloves and cook, stirring, for 30 seconds, or until fragrant. Add the onion and remaining salt. Reduce the heat to medium–low and cook, stirring occasionally, for 20–25 minutes, until golden brown. Add the ginger and garlic and cook, stirring, for about 30 seconds, until fragrant.

Add the lamb and yoghurt mixture, chilli powder, paprika and turmeric to the pan. Mix well and bring to the boil over medium heat. Reduce the heat to low and cook, covered, for 1¼–1½ hours, until the lamb is tender. Stir in the coriander and garam masala and season, to taste.

Serve with paratha on the side.

Lamb kofta curry
India

2 tablespoons ghee or oil

1 onion, thinly sliced

2 garlic cloves, crushed

2 cm (¾ in) piece ginger, finely grated

¼ teaspoon cumin seeds

400 g (14 oz) tin crushed tomatoes

1 teaspoon ground coriander

½ teaspoon chilli powder

1 teaspoon Garam masala (see page 218 or use store-bought)

250 ml (8½ fl oz/1 cup) coconut milk (see note)

steamed basmati rice (see page 178), to serve

Keema naan (see page 196), to serve

plain yoghurt, to serve

Kofta

500 g (1 lb 2 oz) minced (ground) lamb

1 small onion, finely chopped

2 garlic cloves, crushed

1 cm (½ in) piece ginger, finely grated

½ teaspoon Garam masala (see page 218 or use store-bought)

25 g (1 oz/⅓ cup) fresh breadcrumbs

large handful mint leaves, chopped

large handful coriander (cilantro) leaves, chopped, plus extra to serve

SERVES 4

To make the kofta, place all the ingredients in a large bowl. Season with salt and pepper and mix well. Roll tablespoonfuls of the mixture into balls with damp hands.

Heat a non-stick frying pan over medium heat. Add 1 tablespoon of the ghee or oil and, working in batches, cook the kofta, stirring gently, for 4–5 minutes, until lightly browned all over. Transfer to a plate.

Return the pan to the heat and add the remaining 1 tablespoon of ghee or oil. Add the onion, garlic, ginger and cumin seeds and cook for 4–5 minutes, until the onion is soft. Stir in the tomato, remaining spices and coconut milk. Bring to the boil, then reduce the heat and simmer gently for 5 minutes. Return the kofta to the pan and cook for a further 10 minutes, or until the kofta are cooked through and the sauce is thickened slightly.

Serve the curry with steamed basmati rice, keema naan and yoghurt on the side.

NOTE: IF YOU PREFER A SLIGHTLY LESS RICH SAUCE, USE HALF COCONUT MILK AND HALF PLAIN YOGHURT.

Fijian lamb curry

Fiji

60 ml (2 fl oz/¼ cup) vegetable oil

1.5 kg (3 lb 5 oz) lamb shoulder chops, trimmed

8 fresh curry leaves

3 teaspoons cumin seeds

3 teaspoons finely grated fresh turmeric

2 teaspoons black mustard seeds

2 teaspoons fennel seeds

4 whole cloves

4 cardamom pods

2 star anise

1 cinnamon stick

1 large onion, sliced

4 garlic cloves, finely chopped

3 cm (1¼ in) piece ginger peeled and finely grated

2 long green chillies, chopped

1 medium tomato, chopped

1 large potato, chopped

3 teaspoons Garam masala (see page 218 or use store-bought)

½ bunch coriander (cilantro), chopped

Roti canai (see page 199), to serve

SERVES 6–8

Heat 2 tablespoons of the oil in a large heavy-based saucepan over medium heat. Add the chops and brown them on both sides, then remove to a plate. Add the remaining oil, curry leaves and spices and cook, stirring, for 2 minutes. Reduce the heat to low and add the onion, garlic, ginger and chilli and cook, stirring occasionally, for 5–6 minutes, until the onion has softened.

Return the lamb to the pan and pour in 375 ml (12½ fl oz/1½ cups) water. Add the tomato and simmer over low heat for 1½ hours, adding more water during cooking to maintain a saucy consistency.

Add the potato and another 125 ml (4 fl oz/½ cup) water and cook for a further 15–20 minutes until the potato is tender.

Season to taste with salt and sprinkle over the garam masala and coriander. Serve with roti on the side.

Bhuna gosht

India

4 teaspoons coriander seeds

2 teaspoons cumin seeds

⅛ teaspoon peppercorns

2 cm (¾ in) piece cinnamon stick

2 teaspoons fenugreek seeds

2 small hot dried chillies

3 cardamom pods, smashed and
seeds removed

¼ teaspoon ground turmeric

1 large onion, roughly chopped

4 garlic cloves

3.5 cm (1½ in) piece ginger, roughly
chopped

1 long red chilli (seeded if you prefer
less heat), roughly chopped

1 kg (2 lb 3 oz) boneless lamb shoulder,
cut into 2.5 cm (1 in) pieces

60 g (2 oz/¼ cup) plain yoghurt, plus
extra to serve

3 tablespoons ghee, mustard oil or
vegetable oil

400 g (14 oz) tin crushed tomatoes

½ teaspoon Garam masala (see page 218
or use store-bought)

coriander (cilantro) sprigs, to serve

Chapattis (see page 190), to serve

SERVES 4

Toast the coriander, cumin, peppercorns, cinnamon and fenugreek seeds separately in a dry frying pan over medium heat for 30 seconds, or until fragrant. Transfer to a mortar and pestle or spice grinder, along with the dried chillies, cardamom seeds and turmeric and pound or grind to a fine powder.

Blend or process the onion, garlic, ginger and chilli until puréed. Add a little water to get the mixture moving if needed.

Combine the lamb, yoghurt, onion mixture and spices in a large bowl. Cover, then refrigerate and marinate for at least 2 hours.

Heat the ghee or oil in a heavy-based saucepan over medium–high heat. Add the meat, along with the marinade and cook, stirring occasionally, for 3–4 minutes, until the meat changes colour (be careful not to burn the spices). Add the tomato and enough water to come half way up the height of the meat.

Bring to the boil, then reduce the heat to low. Cover and cook, stirring occasionally, for 1½ hours, until the meat is tender. Remove the lid and continue to cook, uncovered, for a further 15–20 minutes, until the sauce has reduced and thickened enough to coat the meat (the end result should be quite dry). Stir in the garam masala.

Scatter the curry with coriander and serve with chapattis and the extra yoghurt on the side.

Curried lamb pies

U.K.

600 g (1 lb 5 oz) Lamb massaman (see page 156)

Dough

500 g (1 lb 2 oz) plain (all-purpose) flour, plus extra for dusting

2 teaspoons baking powder

1 teaspoon ground turmeric

½ teaspoon cumin seeds

80 ml (2½ fl oz/⅓ cup) vegetable oil

1 free-range egg

40 g (1½ oz) butter, melted, plus extra for greasing

2 tablespoons milk

MAKES 6

To make the dough, sift the flour, baking powder and turmeric into a large bowl. Stir in the cumin seeds. In a jug, combine the oil, egg, butter and 160 ml (5½ fl oz) water. Pour into the flour mixture and mix until combined. Cover with a damp cloth and set aside for 10 minutes.

Turn the dough out onto a lightly floured work surface and knead for 2–3 minutes, until smooth and no longer sticky. Wrap the dough in plastic wrap and leave to rest at room temperature for 2 hours. You can also make the dough in advance and leave it in the fridge, just remember to bring it to room temperature before rolling out.

Preheat the oven to 180°C (350°F) fan-forced. Grease a large (Texan) 6-hole muffin tin with butter.

Set aside one quarter of the dough. Divide the remaining dough into six equal portions. Roll each portion out on a lightly floured work surface into 15 cm (6 in) circles. Line the prepared muffin tin with the pastry circles. Spoon 100 g (3½ oz) portions of the curry into the lined muffin holes. Divide the reserved dough into 6 equal portions and roll into 10 cm (4 in) circles for the lids. Place over the top of the pies and pinch the edges to seal or fold over decoratively.

Brush the tops of the pies with the milk and snip a breathing hole in the top of each pie with kitchen scissors.

Bake for 25–30 minutes, until the pastry is golden.

NOTE: ANY CURRY CAN BE TRANSFORMED INTO DELICIOUS PIES. THIS DOUGH IS SLIGHTLY BREAD-LIKE IN CONSISTENCY AND HOLDS THE JUICES OF EVEN WET CURRIES REALLY WELL.

Kashmiri goat curry
India

1 kg (2 lb 3 oz) boneless goat shoulder or leg, chopped into 3–4 cm (1¼–1½ in) chunks

250 g (9 oz/1 cup) plain yoghurt

1 tablespoon Kashmiri chilli powder

1 tablespoon ground coriander

1 tablespoon ground cumin

2 teaspoons ground turmeric

4 cm (1½ in) piece ginger, peeled and finely grated

8 garlic cloves, finely chopped

Curry

60 ml (2 fl oz/¼ cup) vegetable oil

2 red onions, thinly sliced

5 whole cloves

5 cardamom pods

3 long green chillies, chopped

½ teaspoon ground fennel seeds

3 fresh bay leaves (preferably Indian)

4 tomatoes, finely chopped or blended

2 teaspoons Garam masala (see page 218 or use store-bought)

1 teaspoon salt

coriander (cilantro) leaves, to serve

steamed basmati rice (see page 178) or Paratha (see page 191), to serve

SERVES 4

Combine the goat, yoghurt, chilli powder, coriander, cumin, turmeric, ginger and garlic in a large bowl. Set aside to marinate in the fridge for at least 3 hours or preferably overnight.

To make the curry, heat the oil in a large heavy-based saucepan over medium heat. Add the onion, cloves, cardamom, chillies, fennel and bay leaves and cook, stirring occasionally, for 5 minutes, or until the onion softens. Add the tomato and simmer for 2–3 minutes, until the oil starts to separate a little.

Increase the heat and add the goat, along with its marinade. Stir, allowing the goat to slightly brown, then pour 250 ml (8½ fl oz/1 cup) water into the pan. Cover and simmer gently for 35–40 minutes, until the goat is tender. You can add more water if the sauce starts to dry out. Add the garam masala and salt and stir through.

Scatter the curry with coriander leaves and serve with steamed basmati rice or paratha.

1 tablespoon ground coriander

1 teaspoon ground cumin

1 teaspoon ground cinnamon

½ teaspoon ground cardamom

½ teaspoon freshly ground black pepper

2 dried red chillies, soaked in hot water
for 15 minutes, drained

4 long green chillies, roughly chopped

handful mint leaves, roughly chopped

handful coriander (cilantro) leaves,
roughly chopped

2.5 cm (1 in) piece ginger, finely grated

6 garlic cloves, crushed,

1 tablespoon dried fenugreek leaves

1 teaspoon ground turmeric

1 tablespoon vegetable oil

600 g (1 lb 5 oz) boneless lamb shoulder,
cut into 4 cm (1½ in) pieces

3 tablespoons ghee

3 onions, thickly sliced

1 large tomato, roughly chopped

65 g (2¼ oz/⅓ cup) masoor dal (split red
lentils), well rinsed

65 g (2¼ oz/⅓ cup) moong dal (skinned
split mung beans), well rinsed

1 small eggplant (aubergine), cut into
1.5 cm (½ in) pieces

300 g (10½ oz) pumpkin (winter squash),
deseeded and cut into 2 cm (¾ in)
pieces

2 teaspoons tamarind purée

steamed basmati rice (see page 178),
to serve

SERVES 4

Lamb dhansak
India

Roast the coriander, cumin, cinnamon, cardamom and black pepper in a dry frying pan over medium heat for about 30 seconds, until fragrant.

Blend or process the soaked chillies, green chillies, mint leaves, coriander leaves, ginger, garlic, fenugreek leaves, turmeric, roasted spices and oil until puréed. Add a little water to get the mixture moving if necessary.

Combine the lamb and spice purée in a large bowl. Cover and set aside in the fridge to marinate for at least 2 hours or overnight.

Heat the ghee in a large heavy-based saucepan over medium–high heat. Add the onion, then reduce the heat to medium and cook, stirring occasionally, for 12–15 minutes, until golden. Remove half the onion and set aside for garnish. Increase the heat to medium–high again, then add the lamb and cook, stirring occasionally, for 8–10 minutes, until changed in colour. Add the tomato and cook, stirring, for 2–3 minutes, then stir in the masoor dal, moong dal, eggplant and pumpkin. Pour over enough water to cover.

Bring to the boil, then reduce the heat to low. Cover and cook, stirring often, for 1–1½ hours, until the meat is tender. Stir in the tamarind purée and season, to taste. Add extra boiling water along the way as the lentils cook and thicken the sauce – the final consistency should be quite thick.

Reheat the reserved onion in a small saucepan.

Serve the curry topped with the onion and with steamed basmati rice on the side.

Rice & bread

Perfect steamed rice

400 g (14 oz/2 cups) basmati or jasmine rice, well rinsed

SERVES 6

Place the rice and 750 ml (25¼ fl oz/3 cups) water in a heavy-based saucepan. Bring to the boil over high heat, cover and reduce the heat to low. Cook for 10 minutes then, without lifting the lid, remove from the heat and stand for a further 10 minutes for the rice to steam and finish cooking.

Gently separate the grains with a fork and serve.

1 tablespoon peanut (ground nut) oil

400 g (14 oz/2 cups) jasmine rice, rinsed and drained

2 garlic cloves, crushed

1 lemongrass stalk, pale section only, bruised and cut into 6 cm (2½ in) lengths

2 kaffir lime leaves, torn

4 cm (1½ in) piece ginger, thickly sliced

750 ml (25½ fl oz/3 cups) vegetable or chicken stock or water

SERVES 6–8

Fragrant jasmine rice
Thailand

Heat the peanut oil in a large heavy-based saucepan over medium–high heat, add the rice and garlic and stir for about 30 seconds, until well combined and the garlic is fragrant. Add the lemongrass, lime leaves, ginger and stock or water and bring to the boil, stirring occasionally. Cover with a lid, reduce the heat to low and simmer for 12 minutes.

Turn off the heat and sit, without removing the lid, for 10 minutes. Fluff gently with a fork, remove the whole aromatics if you like and serve.

Jollof rice
West Africa

1 x 400 g (14 oz) tin peeled tomatoes

2 red onions, roughly chopped

1 large red capsicum (bell pepper), roughly chopped

2 garlic cloves

3 tablespoons vegetable oil

2 tablespoons tomato paste (concentrated purée)

1 scotch bonnet or habanero chilli, chopped (seeded if you prefer less heat)

1 teaspoon all-purpose curry powder

1 teaspoon smoked paprika

½ teaspoon white pepper

½ teaspoon dried thyme

¾ teaspoon salt

400 g (14 oz/2 cups) long-grain rice, rinsed and drained

750 ml (25½ fl oz/3 cups) vegetable stock or water

SERVES 6–8

Blend or process the tomato, onion, capsicum and garlic until smooth.

Heat the oil in a large heavy-based saucepan over medium heat and add the puréed tomato mixture, tomato paste, chilli, curry powder, paprika, pepper and thyme. Bring to the boil, then reduce the heat and simmer, stirring frequently (be careful as the mixture will initially sputter), for 25–30 minutes, until the sauce is reduced and thick.

Add the salt, rice and stock, return to the boil over medium heat, then cover, reduce the heat again and simmer gently, stirring occasionally, for 25–30 minutes, until the rice is just tender. Add a little more boiling water as you go if the mixture becomes too dry.

Turn off the heat and let sit with the lid on for 10 minutes. Stir the rice gently with a fork to separate the grains and serve.

Kashmiri pilau
Kashmir

pinch of saffron threads

3 tablespoons ghee

4 green cardamom pods, bruised

1 cinnamon stick

1 small red chilli, split lengthways

1 small bay leaf (preferably Indian)

3 whole cloves

½ teaspoon fennel seeds

2 cm (¾ in) piece ginger, finely grated

400 g (14 oz/2 cups) basmati rice

750 ml (25½ fl oz/3 cups) chicken stock

3 tablespoons cashew nuts

3 tablespoons almonds, roughly chopped

1 large onion, thinly sliced

55 g (2 oz/⅓ cup) currants

SERVES 6–8

Place the saffron and 60 ml (2 fl oz/¼ cup) warm water in a small bowl. Set aside for 10 minutes to soak.

Heat 1 tablespoon of the ghee in a large heavy-based saucepan over medium–high heat. Add the cardamom, cinnamon, chilli, bay leaf, cloves, fennel and ginger and stir for about 1 minute, until fragrant. Add the rice and saffron water and stir until well combined, then add the chicken stock and bring to the boil, stirring occasionally. Reduce the heat to low, cover and cook for 10 minutes. Turn off the heat and let sit with the lid on for 10 minutes.

Meanwhile, heat the remaining 2 tablespoons of ghee in a large saucepan over medium–high heat. Add the cashew nuts and almonds and cook, stirring, for 1–2 minutes, until golden. Using a slotted spoon, transfer the nuts to a plate lined with paper towel, leaving as much ghee in the pan as possible. Add the onion and a good pinch of salt to the pan and cook, stirring often, for 8–10 minutes, until golden.

Fluff the rice gently with a fork, remove the whole spices if you like and stir in the currants. Season to taste with salt and pepper. Transfer the rice to a serving plate, scatter with the nuts and onion and serve.

Simple saffron rice

India

large pinch of saffron threads

3 tablespoons ghee or butter

400 g (14 oz/2 cups) basmati rice, rinsed

750 ml (25½ fl oz/3 cups) vegetable or
chicken stock

SERVES 6–8

Place the saffron threads in a small bowl and add 3 tablespoons warm water. Set aside to infuse for 10 minutes.

Heat the ghee or butter in a large heavy-based saucepan over medium–high heat, add the rice and stir until well combined. Add the stock and saffron mixture and bring to the boil, stirring occasionally. Cover with a lid, reduce the heat to low and simmer for 10 minutes.

Turn off the heat and sit, without removing the lid, for 10 minutes. Fluff gently with a fork and serve.

2 tablespoons ghee

3 Asian shallots, thinly sliced

1 sprig curry leaves

2 garlic cloves, crushed

4 green cardamom pods, bruised

1 cinnamon stick

large pinch of saffron threads

400 g (14 oz/2 cups) basmati rice, rinsed

800 ml (27 fl oz) chicken stock or water

SERVES 6–8

Heat the ghee in a large heavy-based saucepan over medium–high heat. Add the shallot and cook, stirring, for 4–5 minutes, until golden. Add the curry leaves, garlic, cardamom, cinnamon and saffron and stir for about 1 minute, until fragrant. Add the rice and stir until well combined, then add the chicken stock and bring to a simmer, stirring occasionally. Cover with a lid, reduce the heat to low and cook for 10 minutes. Turn off the heat and sit, without removing the lid, for 10 minutes.

Alternatively, preheat the oven to 160°C (320°F) fan-forced. Melt the ghee in a large heavy-based flameproof casserole dish over medium heat, then add the shallot and cook until golden. Stir through the spices until fragrant, then add the rice and stir until well combined. Add the stock and bring to the boil, then cover and cook in the oven for 15–20 minutes, until the rice is tender.

Remove the whole spices, fluff gently with a fork and serve.

120 ml (4 fl oz) olive or vegetable oil

1 large onion, finely chopped

850 g (1 lb 14 oz) boneless lamb shoulder, chopped into 2.5 cm (1 in) chunks

4 garlic cloves, finely chopped

3 teaspoon salt

750 g (1 lb 11 oz) good-quality basmati rice, soaked for at least 4 hours or overnight

2 large carrots, chopped into batons

1 tablespoon sugar

75 g (2¾ oz) sultanas (golden raisins)

1 teaspoon cumin seeds

½ teaspoon ground cardamom

40 g (1½ oz/¼ cup) shelled pistachio nuts

70 g (2½ oz/½ cup) slivered almonds

Quick garam masala

12 cardamom pods, seeds removed and pods discarded

2 dried bay leaves

1 cinnamon stick

8 whole cloves

SERVES 6

Lamb biryani
Afghanistan

To make the quick garam masala, grind all the ingredients together in a spice grinder. Set aside.

Heat half the oil in a large heavy-based saucepan over low heat. Add the onion and cook, stirring occasionally, for 10 minutes, until soft and golden. Increase the heat to high, add the lamb and brown on all sides. Add the garlic and salt and cook, stirring, for 1 minute. Pour in 2 litres (68 fl oz/8 cups) water, then reduce the heat to low and simmer for 2 hours, regularly skimming the fat off the surface with a spoon.

Bring a large saucepan of water to the boil. Drain the soaked rice and add to the boiling water. Cook for 5 minutes, then drain and set aside.

Heat 2 tablespoons of the remaining oil in a frying pan over medium heat. And the carrot and cook for 2 minutes. Sprinkle over the sugar and stir for 2–3 minutes, until the carrot is soft and glazed. Add the sultanas and cumin seeds and cook, stirring, for 2–3 minutes until softened. Sprinkle over the ground cardamom.

Heat the remaining oil in a small frying pan over medium heat. Add the nuts and gently cook, stirring frequently, until golden. Remove from the heat and set aside.

Put the rice into a large stockpot and strain over the warm lamb mixture. Sprinkle the quick garam masala over the top. Poke holes in the rice with the handle of a wooden spoon to help the rice steam, then spoon over the carrot mixture. Cover the pot with a clean tea towel and place the lid on top.

Heat the pot over low heat and allow to steam for 5 minutes. Remove from the heat and leave the rice to stand for 5 minutes.

Layer the rice and carrot on a serving platter with the lamb. Sprinkle over the nuts and serve straight away.

Vegetable biryani

India

300 g (10½ oz/1½ cups) basmati
  rice, rinsed
80 ml (2½ fl oz/⅓ cup) vegetable oil
1 cinnamon stick
5 whole cloves
5 cardamom pods, bruised
1 black cardamom pod, bruised (optional)
10 curry leaves
1 onion, thinly sliced
1 long green chilli, thinly sliced
4 garlic cloves, crushed
3 cm (1¼ in) piece ginger, finely grated
½ teaspoon chilli powder
2 teaspoons ground coriander
1 teaspoon ground fennel seeds
1 teaspoon cumin seeds
½ teaspoon ground turmeric
2 tomatoes, finely chopped
2 carrots, cut into 5 cm (2 in) batons
125 g (4½ oz) cauliflower florets
pinch of saffron threads
200 ml (7 fl oz) coconut milk
125 g (4½ oz) green beans, trimmed
  and halved

To serve

chopped coriander (cilantro) leaves
75 g (2¾ oz/½ cup) cashew nuts, toasted
2 tablespoons raisins
mint leaves
Garam masala (see page 218 or use
  store-bought) (optional)
lemon wedges

SERVES 4–6

Soak the rice in 250 ml (8½ fl oz/1 cup) water for 30 minutes. Drain.

Heat the oil in a large heavy-based saucepan over medium–high heat. Add the cinnamon, cloves, cardamom and curry leaves and cook for 1–2 minutes, until they start to crackle. Add the onion, then reduce the heat to low and cook for 10 minutes, until soft and slightly golden. Add the chilli, garlic and ginger and cook, stirring, for 2 minutes. Stir in the chilli powder, ground coriander, fennel seeds, cumin seeds and ground turmeric, and cook for 1 minute, then add the tomato and cook, stirring, for 5 minutes. Add the drained rice and stir to coat in the spices, then add the carrot and cauliflower.

In a small bowl, combine the saffron and coconut milk, then add to the pan, along with enough water to just cover the rice, carrot and cauliflower, about 350 ml (12 fl oz). Cover and simmer for 15–20 minutes, until the rice has absorbed the liquid. Add the beans, turn off the heat and stand, covered, for a further 5–8 minutes, until the beans are tender and the rice is cooked through. Season with salt to taste.

Transfer the biryani to a serving platter and scatter over the coriander, cashew nuts, raisins and mint leaves. Sprinkle with garam masala, if using, and serve with lemon wedges for squeezing over.

Chapattis
India

225 g (8 oz/1½ cups) wholemeal (whole-wheat) flour or atta flour (see note), plus extra for dusting
½ teaspoon salt
1 tablespoon ghee
melted butter, to brush (optional)

MAKES 8

Sift the flour and salt into a medium bowl. Add the ghee and rub in with your fingertips until the mixture resembles fine breadcrumbs. Make a well in the centre and add almost 125 ml (4 fl oz/½ cup) lukewarm water. Mix until you have a firmish dough, adding the remaining water if necessary. Cover and set aside to rest for 10 minutes.

Turn the dough out onto a lightly floured work surface and knead for 1–2 minutes, until smooth. Divide the dough into eight equal-sized portions, then form each portion into a ball. Place the dough in a single layer on a baking tray. Cover with plastic wrap and set aside to rest for 30 minutes, or for as long as overnight. Rest in the fridge if the weather is warm.

Working with one ball of dough at a time, roll out on a lightly floured work surface into a thin 16 cm (6¼ in) circle. Repeat with the remaining dough.

Heat a large non-stick frying pan or heavy cast-iron griddle over medium–high heat. Once the frying pan is smoking hot, add a circle of dough to the pan and cook, lightly pressing the dough all over with a clean dry tea towel in a dabbing motion, for about 1 minute, or until the bottom surface is lightly browned in spots and starting to bubble. Adjust the heat if necessary. Flip the chapattis over and cook for 30–60 seconds, until cooked through. Remove from the pan and brush with melted butter if you like. Transfer to a plate and cover with a clean tea towel to keep warm and prevent the chapattis from drying out. Repeat with the remaining dough.

Serve straight away, or reheat briefly in a warm frying pan just before serving.

NOTES: ATTA FLOUR IS AVAILABLE FROM INDIAN GROCERY STORES AND SOME SUPERMARKETS.

YOU CAN ALSO COOK CHAPATTIS ON A BARBECUE HOTPLATE, ALLOWING YOU TO COOK SEVERAL AT ONCE.

Paratha
India

110 g (4 oz/¾ cup) wholemeal (whole-wheat) flour

110 g (4 oz/¾ cup) plain (all-purpose) flour

½ teaspoon salt

¼ teaspoon baking powder

1 tablespoon ghee, plus extra, melted, for brushing and cooking

½ teaspoon nigella seeds

MAKES 8

Sift the flours, salt and baking powder into a medium bowl. Add the ghee and rub in with your fingertips until the mixture resembles fine breadcrumbs. Make a well in the centre and add the nigella seeds and almost 125 ml (4 fl oz/½ cup) water. Mix until you have a soft dough, adding the remaining water if necessary. Cover and set aside to rest for 10 minutes.

Turn the dough out onto a lightly floured work surface and knead for 1–2 minutes, until smooth. Divide the dough into eight equal-sized portions, then form each portion into a ball. Place the dough in a single layer on a baking tray. Cover with plastic wrap or a clean damp tea towel and set aside to rest for 30 minutes.

Working with one ball of dough at a time, roll out on a lightly floured work surface into a thin 17 cm (6¾ in) circle. Brush lightly with extra melted ghee, then fold in half, brush with more ghee and fold again so that the circle is folded into quarters. Set aside in a single layer and cover with a tea towel while you roll the remaining dough.

Roll out each folded portion of dough to a triangle shape about 2 mm (⅛ in) thick.

Heat a large non-stick frying pan or heavy cast-iron griddle over medium heat. Working with one paratha at a time, brush the top with more melted ghee and cook, ghee-side down, lightly pressing all over with a clean dry tea towel, for 1–2 minutes, until golden brown in spots (adjust the heat if necessary). Brush the top with ghee, then flip over and cook for a further 30–60 seconds, until golden and cooked through. Stack the paratha on a plate and cover with a clean tea towel to keep warm and prevent them drying out.

Serve straight away, or reheat briefly in a warm frying pan just before serving.

NOTE: YOU CAN ALSO COOK PARATHA ON A BARBECUE HOTPLATE, ALLOWING YOU TO COOK SEVERAL AT ONCE.

300 g (10½ oz/2 cups) teff flour (see notes)
½ teaspoon dried instant yeast
½ teaspoon baking powder
ghee or vegetable oil, for cooking

MAKES 8–10

Injera
Ethiopia

Combine the flour, yeast and 750 ml (25½ fl oz/3 cups) water in a large mixing bowl. Loosely cover the bowl with plastic wrap or a clean tea towel and let the mixture sit undisturbed at room temperature for at least 2–3 hours, but ideally overnight and even up to 2–3 days to really allow the mixture to bubble and ferment. When ready, the mixture will smell slightly sweet and fermented and will taste sour. (The longer it ferments, the deeper the flavour will be). Without disturbing the mixture, gently pour off as much of the separated liquid as possible. A slightly thicker batter will remain in the bowl.

Bring 250 ml (8½ fl oz/1 cup) water to the boil in a small saucepan over medium heat. Stir in 125 ml (4 fl oz/½ cup) of the injera batter. Whisk constantly for about 30 seconds or until the mixture boils and thickens.

Stir the thickened batter back into the remaining fermented batter, along with the baking powder. If necessary, add a little water to thin the batter to the consistency of thin cream. Pour the batter into a jug.

Heat a large non-stick frying pan with a lid over medium heat. Add a small knob of ghee or a little oil to the frying pan and wipe round with clean paper towel. Pour about 100 ml (3½ fl oz) of the batter into the pan in a spiral motion, starting on the outside and working towards the centre to cover the entire surface. Cook for 1–2 minutes, or until all the bubbles have popped. Cover the frying pan with a lid and cook for a further 1–2 minutes, or until the bread is cooked through and the edges start to curl. Carefully remove the injera with a spatula, set aside on a plate and cover with a clean tea towel. Repeat with the remaining mixture, then roll up and serve immediately.

NOTES: TEFF FLOUR IS AVAILABLE FROM HEALTH-FOOD STORES AND SOME SUPERMARKETS IN THE HEALTH-FOOD AISLE.

THE BATTER CAN BE MADE WITH HALF TEFF AND HALF PLAIN (ALL-PURPOSE) FLOUR FOR A LIGHTER BREAD.

Simple naan
India

80 g (2¾ oz/⅓ cup) plain yoghurt
1½ teaspoons dried instant yeast
450 g (1 lb/3 cups) plain (all-purpose) flour,
    plus extra for dusting
1 teaspoon salt
½ teaspoon baking powder
60 ml (2 fl oz/¼ cup) melted ghee,
    plus extra to brush
½ teaspoon nigella seeds

MAKES 6

Mix the yoghurt and 250 ml (8½ fl oz/1 cup) warm water in a large bowl. Stir in the yeast, then add the flour, salt, baking powder and ghee. Mix with your hands to form a soft, sticky dough. Cover and set aside for 20 minutes.

Turn the dough out onto a floured work surface and knead for 1–2 minutes, until quite smooth. Cover and set aside in a warm place for 2–3 hours, until nearly doubled in size.

Preheat the oven to 250°C (480°F) fan-forced (or the hottest your oven will go). Place two baking trays in the oven to heat up. Gently lift the dough (so as not to squish all the air out) from the bowl and place on a well-floured work surface. Cut the dough into six wedges.

With floured hands, gently pat and stretch each wedge into a 15 cm (6 in) circle, keeping them thin in the centre and thicker around the edge. Gently brush with ghee.

Working in batches, carefully transfer the dough circles to the hot trays, pulling one side outwards or downwards to form the classic naan teardrop shape. Bake for 6–7 minutes, until golden brown in spots and the naan is cooked through. Stack on a plate and cover with a clean tea towel to keep warm and to prevent the naan from drying out.

Alternatively, to cook the naan in a frying pan, heat a large non-stick frying pan or heavy cast-iron griddle over medium heat. Working with one piece of dough at a time, brush the top with melted ghee, then transfer to the hot pan, ghee-side down, stretching the dough into a teardrop shape as you go. Cook for 2–3 minutes, until golden brown in spots, adjusting the heat if necessary. Brush the top with ghee, flip over and cook for a further 30–60 seconds, until golden and cooked through.

Serve immediately brushed with a little more ghee and sprinkled with nigella seeds.

NOTE: FOR GARLIC NAAN, WARM A CLOVE OF CRUSHED GARLIC WITH THE EXTRA MELTED GHEE IN A SMALL SAUCEPAN BEFORE BRUSHING OVER THE NAAN.

Keema naan
India

Prepare the naan dough. While the dough is proving, prepare the rest of the ingredients.

Heat the ghee in a frying pan over medium heat. Add the onion, ginger and garlic and cook, stirring occasionally, for 4–5 minutes, until soft and fragrant. Add the tomato paste, turmeric and chilli and cook, stirring, for a further 2–3 minutes, to cook out the tomato paste.

Increase the heat to medium–high and add the lamb and salt. Cook, stirring, for 3–4 minutes, until the meat changes colour. Add the yoghurt and 60 ml (2 fl oz/¼ cup) water, then stir and bring to the boil. Simmer, uncovered, for 3–4 minutes, until most of the liquid evaporates. Remove from the heat, stir in the garam masala and season to taste with a little salt and freshly ground black pepper, then set aside to cool. Once cool, stir through the coriander and divide the mixture into six equal-sized portions.

Preheat the oven to 250°C (480°F) fan-forced (or the hottest your oven will go). Place two baking trays in the oven to heat up. Gently lift the dough (so as not to squish all the air out) from the bowl and place on a well-floured work surface. Cut the dough into six pieces.

Working with one piece of dough at a time, roll the dough out on a lightly floured work surface into a 15 cm (6 in) circle. Spoon one portion of the filling in the centre of the dough, spread it out a little, then bring in the edge of the dough to enclose the filling. Pinch the edges to seal, then flatten the dough with your hands slightly and gently roll, dusting with a little more flour if necessary, into an oval shape about 20 cm (8 in) long. You want the naan to be thin, but not so thin that the filling breaks through. Repeat with the remaining dough and filling.

Brush each naan with ghee, then transfer to the hot trays and cook, in batches if necessary, for 6–7 minutes, until golden and cooked through. Serve immediately with a little extra ghee brushed over the top..

1 x quantity Simple naan dough (see page 194)

1 tablespoon ghee, plus extra, melted, for brushing

1 small onion, finely chopped

2 cm (¾ in) piece ginger, finely grated

2 garlic cloves, crushed

2 tablespoons tomato paste (concentrated purée)

½ teaspoon ground turmeric

½ teaspoon chilli powder

200 g (7 oz) lean minced (ground) lamb

½ teaspoon salt

3 tablespoons plain yoghurt

½ teaspoon Garam masala (see page 218 or use store-bought)

3 tablespoons chopped coriander (cilantro)

MAKES 6

Roti canai

Malaysia

450 g (1 lb/3 cups) plain (all-purpose) flour,
plus extra for dusting

1 teaspoon salt

1 free-range egg

vegetable oil

MAKES 10

Combine the flour and salt in a large bowl. Whisk 250 ml (8½ fl oz/1 cup) water and the egg in a separate bowl, then pour into the flour. Using your hands, mix to form a soft dough, then cover with plastic wrap or a clean tea towel and set aside for 10 minutes.

Turn the dough out onto a floured work surface and knead for 2–3 minutes, to form a soft elastic dough.

Roll the dough into a cylinder and divide into 10 even-sized pieces. Knead each piece a few times until smooth, then roll into a ball. Place the balls in a shallow baking dish and cover completely with oil. Cover with plastic wrap or a clean tea towel and leave to rest at room temperature for at least 3 hours, or preferably overnight. Rest in the fridge if the weather is warm, but bring to room temperature before cooking.

Oil a clean work surface with a little of the oil from the rested dough. Working with one ball of dough at a time, flatten the dough with the palm of your hand. Working from the edge, gently and gradually stretch the dough outwards as far and as thinly as you can, to roughly the thickness of a sheet of paper and 30 cm (12 in) square. It should be quite transparent. You may get a few holes, but this is okay.

Lift one-third of the dough over the remaining two-thirds. Don't be afraid to gently stretch out the edges – they won't stick together. Fold in the short sides in the same manner to end up with a squarish shape. Gently roll the dough with a rolling pin to enlarge the roti slightly – it should be about 17 cm (6¾ in) square. Repeat with the remaining dough.

Heat a heavy non-stick frying pan over medium–high heat. Cook the roti one at a time for 1½–2 minutes each side, until golden brown. Slide the bread onto a chopping board and carefully ruffle and bunch up the roti so it becomes flaky. Serve warm.

Masala dosa
India

Place the rice in a medium bowl and cover with cold water. Place the urad dal and fenugreek seeds in a small bowl and cover with cold water. Leave both bowls to soak for at least 4 hours.

Drain both bowls and place the rice and 250 ml (8½ fl oz/1 cup) cold water in a high-powdered blender. Blend for 10 minutes, or until you have a smooth paste. Transfer to a bowl, then repeat with the urad dal mixture and 125 ml (4 fl oz/½ cup) water. Combine the ground urad dal and ground rice, then whisk in enough cold water (you may need up to 1 cup) until you have a fairly thick batter, similar in consistency to pancake batter. Cover the bowl with a clean tea towel and set aside in a warm place for 6–8 hours, until the mixture ferments and a bubbly froth appears on the surface. Stir in the salt.

To make the filling, boil the potatoes for 10–15 minutes, until tender. Drain and lightly crush or roughly dice the potato and set aside. Heat the oil in a large heavy-based frying pan over medium heat. Add the mustard seeds and curry leaves and fry for 1 minute, or until the seeds start to sizzle and pop. Add the onion and cook for 5 minutes, until soft. Add the garlic, chilli, ginger and turmeric and cook, stirring, for 2 minutes. Add the potato and salt and toss well in the spices. Stir through the coriander.

Place a 20 cm (8 in) frying pan over medium heat. Brush the base of the pan with about 1 teaspoon oil. Ladle 125 ml (4 fl oz/½ cup) of the batter into the centre of the pan and, using the back of the ladle, spread it out very thinly in a circular motion. Drizzle 1 teaspoon oil over the top of the batter. Cook for 2–3 minutes, or until the edge is dry and the base is golden and crisp. Flip and cook the other side for 50–60 seconds. Remove to a plate and cover with a clean tea towel. Repeat with the remaining batter.

Evenly spoon the potato filling along the centre of each dosa. Fold the dosa over the filling and serve immediately with green chutney and yoghurt on the side.

440 g (15½ oz/2 cups) short-grain rice, well rinsed
110 g (4 oz/½ cup) split urad dal (white lentils), rinsed
½ teaspoon fenugreek seeds
½ teaspoon salt
sunflower or vegetable oil, for frying
green chutney, to serve
plain yoghurt, to serve

Filling
750 g (1 lb 11 oz) potatoes, peeled
80 ml (2½ fl oz/⅓ cup) sunflower or vegetable oil
1 teaspoon black mustard seeds
2 sprigs curry leaves (about 24 leaves)
1 large onion, finely chopped
2 garlic cloves, crushed
3 long green chillies, finely chopped
3 cm (1¼ in) piece ginger, finely grated
½ teaspoon ground turmeric
½ teaspoon salt, or to taste
handful coriander (cilantro) leaves, chopped

MAKES 8

NOTE: THE DOSA BATTER WILL KEEP IN AN AIRTIGHT CONTAINER IN THE FRIDGE FOR UP TO 1 WEEK.

Basics

Red curry paste
Thailand

1½ teaspoons coriander seeds

1 teaspoon cumin seeds

1 teaspoon white peppercorns

2 teaspoons Thai shrimp paste

½ teaspoon freshly grated nutmeg

6 dried long red chillies, seeded, soaked in warm water for 15 minutes, drained and chopped

2 Asian shallots, chopped

2 lemongrass stalks, pale section only, thinly sliced

5 garlic cloves, roughly chopped

1 tablespoon chopped coriander (cilantro) roots

1 tablespoon sweet paprika

3 kaffir lime leaves, chopped

1 teaspoon finely grated kaffir lime zest or lime zest

1 cm (½ in) piece galangal, peeled and finely chopped or grated

1 teaspoon salt

1 tablespoon peanut (ground nut) oil

MAKES ABOUT 280 G (10 OZ)

Toast the coriander and cumin seeds in a small dry frying pan, shaking the pan constantly, for 30–60 seconds, until fragrant. Set aside to cool, then grind the toasted spices and peppercorns using a mortar and pestle or in a spice grinder until finely ground.

Wrap the shrimp paste in foil and cook in a dry frying pan or under a hot grill (broiler), turning the package every now and then, for 3 minutes, or until fragrant.

Blend the ground spices, shrimp paste, nutmeg and soaked chilli in a blender or the small bowl of a food processor, until combined. Add the remaining ingredients and blend until a smooth paste is formed, scraping down the sides of the blender or processor as necessary. Add a small amount of water to get the mixture moving, if necessary. Alternatively, you can pound the ingredients to a paste using a large mortar and pestle. Start with the hardest ingredients, pounding each until smooth before adding the next.

Divide the curry paste into portions and keep in an airtight container in the fridge for up to 1 week or in the freezer for up to 3 months.

Green curry paste
Thailand

1 teaspoon coriander seeds

1 teaspoon cumin seeds

2 teaspoons Thai shrimp paste

6 long green chillies, roughly chopped

8 small Thai green chillies, roughly chopped

5 spring onions (scallions), roughly chopped

40 g (1¾ oz) chopped coriander (cilantro) stems and roots

2 Asian shallots, chopped

2 lemongrass stalks, pale section only, thinly sliced

2 garlic cloves, roughly chopped

2 cm (¾ in) piece galangal, peeled and finely chopped or grated

1 teaspoon finely grated kaffir lime zest or lime zest

1 tablespoon peanut (ground nut) oil

MAKES ABOUT 360 G (12½ OZ)

Toast the coriander and cumin seeds in a small dry frying pan, shaking the pan constantly, for 30–60 seconds, until fragrant. Set aside to cool, then grind using a mortar and pestle or in a spice grinder until finely ground.

Wrap the shrimp paste in foil and cook in a dry frying pan or under a hot grill (broiler), turning the package every now and then, for 3 minutes, or until fragrant.

Blend the ground spices, shrimp paste and chillies in a blender or the small bowl of a food processor, until combined. Add the remaining ingredients and blend until a smooth paste is formed, scraping down the sides of the blender or processor as necessary. Add a small amount of water to get the mixture moving, if necessary. Alternatively, you can pound the ingredients to a paste using a large mortar and pestle. Start with the hardest ingredients, pounding each until smooth before adding the next.

Divide the curry paste into portions and keep in an airtight container in the fridge for up to 1 week or in the freezer for up to 3 months.

Yellow curry paste
Thailand

1 teaspoon coriander seeds

1 teaspoon cumin seeds

1.5 cm (½ in) piece cinnamon stick

2 dried long red chillies, seeded, soaked in warm water for 15 minutes, drained and chopped

1 teaspoon Thai shrimp paste

2 yellow banana peppers, roughly chopped

3 tablespoons chopped coriander (cilantro) stems and roots

1 small onion, chopped

2 lemongrass stalks, pale section only, thinly sliced

2 cm (¾ in) piece galangal, peeled and finely chopped or grated

1.5 cm (½ in) piece fresh turmeric, roughly chopped

2 garlic cloves, roughly chopped

1 tablespoon peanut (ground nut) oil

MAKES ABOUT 280 G (10 OZ)

Toast the coriander seeds, cumin seeds and cinnamon separately in a small dry frying pan, shaking the pan constantly, for 30–60 seconds, until fragrant. Cool and grind using a mortar and pestle or in a spice grinder until finely ground.

Wrap the shrimp paste in foil and cook in a dry frying pan or under a hot grill (broiler), turning the package every now and then, for 3 minutes, or until fragrant.

Blend the ground spices, shrimp paste and soaked chilli in a blender or the small bowl of a food processor, until combined. Add the remaining ingredients and blend until a smooth paste is formed, scraping down the sides of the blender or processor as necessary. Add a small amount of water to get the mixture moving, if necessary. Alternatively, you can pound the ingredients to a paste using a large mortar and pestle. Start with the hardest ingredients, pounding each until smooth before adding the next.

Divide the curry paste into portions and keep in an airtight container in the fridge for up to 1 week or in the freezer for up to 3 months.

Massaman curry paste

Thailand

2 teaspoons coriander seeds

2 teaspoons cumin seeds

2 cm (¾ in) piece cinnamon stick

½ teaspoon whole cloves

5 Thai cardamom pods (or regular cardamom pods), bruised and seeds removed

3 tablespoons roasted unsalted peanuts

8 dried long red chillies, seeded, soaked in warm water for 15 minutes, drained and chopped

1 onion, roughly chopped

3 lemongrass stalks, pale section only, thinly sliced

1 tablespoon chopped coriander (cilantro) roots

4 cm (1¼ in) piece ginger, chopped

5 garlic cloves, roughly chopped

4 kaffir lime leaves, chopped

1 teaspoon Thai shrimp paste

1 tablespoon peanut (ground nut) oil

¼ teaspoon salt

MAKES ABOUT 280 G (10 OZ)

Preheat the oven to 160°C (320°C) fan-forced.

Toast the coriander and cumin seeds, cinnamon and cloves separately in a small dry frying pan, shaking the pan constantly, for 30–60 seconds, until fragrant. Set aside to cool, then grind with the cardamom seeds and peanuts using a mortar and pestle or spice grinder until finely ground.

Place the soaked chilli, onion, lemongrass, coriander roots, ginger, garlic and lime leaves in a shallow baking dish. Roast, uncovered, for 10–15 minutes, until lightly browned and fragrant.

Wrap the shrimp paste in foil and cook in a dry frying pan or under a hot grill (broiler), turning the package every now and then, for 3 minutes, or until fragrant.

Blend the ground spice mixture and shrimp paste in a blender or the small bowl of a food processor, until combined. Add the roasted mixture, oil and salt and blend until a smooth paste is formed, scraping down the sides of the blender or processor as necessary. Add a small amount of water to get the mixture moving, if necessary. Alternatively, you can pound the ingredients to a paste using a large mortar and pestle. Start with the hardest ingredients, pounding each until smooth before adding the next.

Divide the curry paste into portions and keep in an airtight container in the fridge for up to 1 week or in the freezer for up to 3 months.

Jungle curry paste
Thailand

1½ teaspoons Thai shrimp paste

1 tablespoon coriander seeds

1 teaspoon cumin seeds

3 Asian shallots, peeled

3 garlic cloves, peeled

2 cm (¾ in) piece ginger, chopped

1 stalk lemongrass, peeled, pale section
    only, roughly chopped

1.5 cm (½ in) piece turmeric, finely grated

6 coriander (cilantro) roots, scraped
    and cleaned

1 tablespoon peeled and chopped galangal

grated zest of 1 kaffir lime (or substitute
    2 kaffir lime leaves and 1 teaspoon
    lime zest)

3 long green chillies, seeded

5 green bird's eye chillies

½ teaspoon white peppercorns

1½ teaspoons salt

MAKES ABOUT 200 G (7 OZ)

Wrap the shrimp paste in foil and toast in a dry frying pan over medium heat until fragrant. Remove from the pan and set aside. Add the coriander and cumin seeds to the pan and toast for 2–3 minutes, until fragrant. Transfer the toasted seeds and shrimp paste to a mortar and pestle or the bowl of a food processor, along with the remaining paste ingredients and pound or blitz until you have a paste.

Keep in an airtight container in the fridge for up to 1 week or in the freezer for up to 3 months.

Panang curry paste
Thailand

½ teaspoon freshly grated nutmeg

6 dried long red chillies, seeded, soaked in warm water for 15 minutes, drained and chopped

2 Asian shallots, chopped

2 lemongrass stalks, pale section only, thinly sliced

5 garlic cloves, roughly chopped

1 tablespoon cleaned and chopped coriander (cilantro) roots

1 tablespoon sweet paprika

3 kaffir lime leaves, chopped

1 teaspoon finely grated kaffir lime zest or lime zest

1 cm (½ in) piece fresh galangal, finely chopped or grated

1 teaspoon salt

1 tablespoon peanut (ground nut) oil

MAKES ABOUT 280 G (10 OZ)

Place the ingredients in a blender or the small bowl of a food processor and blend to a smooth paste, scraping down the sides of the blender as necessary. Add a little water to get the mixture moving, if necessary.

Alternatively, pound the ingredients to a paste using a large mortar and pestle, pounding each ingredient until smooth before adding the next.

Divide the curry paste into portions and keep in an airtight container in the fridge for up to 1 week or in the freezer for up to 3 months.

Rendang curry paste
Indonesia

2 onions, roughly chopped

3 garlic cloves

5 cm (2 in) piece fresh ginger, chopped

4 small dried red chillies, soaked in hot water for 15 minutes, drained and coarsely chopped

4 cm (1½ in) piece galangal, grated

1 teaspoon ground coriander

2 teaspoons sweet paprika

2 teaspoons ground cumin

1 teaspoon ground turmeric

1 teaspoon sugar

1½ teaspoons salt

MAKES ABOUT 370 G (13 OZ)

Place all the ingredients in a blender or the small bowl of a food processor and process to make a paste. Add a small amount of water to get the mixture moving, if necessary.

Keep in an airtight container in the fridge for up to 1 week or in the freezer for up to 3 months.

Sambal
Malaysia

60 g (2 oz) ikan bilis (dried anchovies)

80 ml (2½ fl oz) peanut (ground nut) oil

7 long dried red chillies, sliced in half and deseeded

6 Asian shallots, 3 finely chopped, 3 thinly sliced

1 garlic clove, crushed

1 teaspoon Thai shrimp paste

2–3 tablespoons tamarind purée

2–3 teaspoons sugar, to taste

½ teaspoon salt, to taste

MAKES 250 G (9 OZ)

Rinse the dried anchovies and pat dry with paper towel. Heat the oil in a small saucepan over high heat. Add the anchovies and cook, stirring, until golden and crisp. Remove with a slotted spoon and drain on paper towel.

Using a mortar and pestle or food processor, pound or process the chillies, finely chopped shallot, garlic and shrimp paste to a smooth paste.

Reheat the reserved oil from the anchovies over medium heat and cook the chilli paste for 2 minutes, or until fragrant. Add the sliced shallot and the fried anchovies and combine well. Add the tamarind purée, sugar and salt, to taste. Bring to the boil, then reduce the heat to low and simmer for 8–10 minutes, until the sambal has thickened slightly.

Keep in an airtight container in the fridge for up to 1 week or in the freezer for up to 3 months.

Laksa paste
Malaysia

8 small dried red chillies, soaked in warm
     water for 15 minutes, drained and
     coarsely chopped

5 Asian shallots, chopped

3 lemongrass stalks, pale section only,
     peeled and thinly sliced

1 tablespoon belacan (fermented
     shrimp paste)

3 cm (1¼ in) piece fresh galangal, finely
     chopped or grated

1 cm (½ in) piece fresh turmeric, chopped

6 candlenuts or macadamia nuts, chopped

2 garlic cloves

1 teaspoon sweet paprika

MAKES ABOUT 380 G (13½ OZ)

Blend all the ingredients in the small bowl of a food processor or blender to a smooth paste. Add a little water to get the mixture moving, if necessary.

Keep in an airtight container in the fridge for up to 1 week or in the freezer for up to 3 months.

Katsu curry sauce
Japan

2 tablespoons peanut (ground nut) oil
1 small onion, very thinly sliced
3 cm (1¼ in) piece ginger, finely grated
2 garlic cloves, crushed
2 tablespoons plain (all-purpose) flour
1 tablespoon all-purpose curry powder
500 ml (17 fl oz/2 cups) chicken stock
2 tablespoons light soy sauce
2 teaspoons honey, plus extra to taste
1 tablespoon sake
¼ teaspoon sesame oil

MAKES ABOUT 375 G (13 OZ)

Heat the oil in a medium saucepan over medium heat. Add the onion, ginger and garlic and cook, stirring, for 3–4 minutes, until soft. Add the flour and curry powder and cook, stirring, for 1–2 minutes, until fragrant. Gradually whisk in the stock, soy sauce and honey and simmer, whisking occasionally, for 15 minutes, or until thickened. Whisk in the sake and sesame oil, and add a little more honey, to taste, if necessary.

Tandoori curry paste

India

½ small onion, roughly chopped

4 garlic cloves

3 cm (1¼ in) piece ginger, roughly chopped

1 tablespoon ground cumin

3 teaspoons ground coriander

1 teaspoon ground turmeric

1 teaspoon sweet paprika

½ teaspoon chilli powder

1 tablespoon lemon juice

natural tandoori or red food colouring

MAKES ABOUT 200 G (7 OZ)

Blend all the ingredients except the food colouring in a blender or the small bowl of a food processor to make a purée. Add a little water to get the mixture moving, if necessary. Add enough food colouring to make the mixture a deep red colour, about ½ teaspoon.

Store the tandoori paste in an airtight container. Left-over paste will keep for up to 2 weeks in the fridge or 3 months in the freezer.

Vindaloo curry paste
India

3 dried red chillies

60 ml (2 fl oz/¼ cup) coconut vinegar
   or white vinegar

1 tablespoon cumin seeds

1 tablespoon coriander seeds

1 teaspoon fenugreek seeds

½ teaspoon black peppercorns

2 cm (¾ in) piece cinnamon stick

5 cloves

3 cardamom pods, bruised and
   seeds removed

6 garlic cloves, crushed

4 cm (1½ in) piece ginger, roughly
   chopped

3 green chillies, chopped (seeded if you
   prefer a milder curry)

2 tablespoons soft brown sugar

¼ teaspoon freshly ground nutmeg

½ teaspoon ground turmeric

MAKES ABOUT 180 G (6½ OZ)

Soak the chillies in the vinegar and set aside to soften.

Roast the whole spices except the cardamom seeds separately in a dry frying pan over medium heat for about 30 seconds, or until fragrant. Grind with the cardamom seeds in a spice grinder to a fine powder.

Blend or process the soaked chillies and vinegar, garlic, gin green chilli, sugar, nutmeg, turmeric and ground spices until pur

Keep in an airtight container in the fridge for up to 1 week or freezer for up to 3 months.

Garam masala
India

4 small cinnamon sticks

4 bay leaves

3 tablespoons coriander seeds

4 teaspoons cumin seeds

3 teaspoons black peppercorns

2 teaspoons cardamom seeds

2 black cardamom pods, seeds only

1 teaspoon whole cloves

1 teaspoon fennel seeds

1 teaspoon black mustard seeds

1 teaspoon ground nutmeg or mace

MAKES ABOUT 60 G (2 OZ)

dients in a small dry frying pan over low heat
minutes, until fragrant. Transfer to a spice
owder.

in an airtight container in the pantry for

Berbere spice mix
Ethiopia

2 tablespoons cumin seeds

2 tablespoons coriander seeds

1 tablespoon whole black peppercorns

1 tablespoon fenugreek seeds

1½ teaspoons whole allspice berries

2 tablespoons salt

1 tablespoon ground ginger

1½ teaspoons ground cloves

1½ teaspoon freshly grated nutmeg

½–1 tablespoon chilli powder, to taste

MAKES ABOUT 100 G (3½ OZ)

Toast the whole spices separately in a dry frying pan ov
medium heat for 30–60 seconds, until fragrant. Coarsely g
using a mortar and pestle or spice grinder. Stir in the salt, gi
cloves, nutmeg and chilli, and mix well to combine.

Store in an airtight container in the pantry for up to 1 mor

Index

Index

Published in 2018 by Smith Street Books
Collingwood | Melbourne | Australia
smithstreetbooks.com

ISBN: 978-1-925418-78-1

CIP data is available from the National Library of Australia

Publisher: Paul McNally
Project editor and editor: Lucy Heaver, Tusk studio
Introduction text: Patrick Boyle
Recipe development: Caroline Griffiths and Jane O'Shannessy
Cover designer: Andy Warren
Design concept: Astred Hicks
Design layout: Heather Menzies, Studio31 Graphics
Photographer: Chris Middleton
Art director and Stylist: Stephanie Stamatis
Home economists: Caroline Griffiths, Jane O'Shannessy,
Sebastian Nichols and Janine Coster

Printed & bound in China by C&C Offset Printing Co., Ltd.
Book 63
10 9 8 7 6 5 4 3 2 1